AN INSIDE LOOK AT A PERFECT SEASON

TALES FROM THE

AUBURN

2004 Championship Season

RICHARD SCOTT

FOREWORD BY TOMMY TUBERVILLE

SP
SPORTS
PUBLISHING
L.L.C.

www.SportsPublishingLLC.com

ISBN: 1-59670-086-6

Publishers: Peter L. Bannon and Joseph J. Bannon Sr.
Senior managing editor: Susan M. Moyer
Acquisitions editor: John Humenik
Developmental editor: Regina D. Sabbia
Art director: K. Jeffrey Higgerson
Dust jacket design and imaging: Dustin Hubbart
Project manager: Greg Hickman
Photo editor: Erin Linden-Levy
Vice president of sales and marketing: Kevin King
Media and promotions managers: Jonathan Patterson (regional),
    Randy Fouts (national), Maurey Williamson (print)

Printed in the United States of America

Sports Publishing L.L.C.
804 North Neil Street
Champaign, IL 61820

Phone: 1-877-424-2665
Fax: 217-363-2073
www.SportsPublishingLLC.com

To Karen, Colin, and Taylor

Contents

Foreword

Coaching college football hasn't been my only job. I've run a catfish restaurant, taught high school, driven a school bus, worked night security and spent time on the docks while I was a volunteer assistant coach at the University of Miami. The one thing I'm not is a writer, but I know enough to understand our 2004 season at Auburn is worthy of a book.

This was the most special group of players I've been around, from their team chemistry to their unselfishness, their hard work day in, day out, their willingness to take coaching and their ability to focus on one practice at a time, one week at a time, one game at a time. They didn't let anything stop them from being the best they could be.

This was a team that truly pulled together in a unique way. The older players led, the younger players followed, and together they defined the word "team" in every sense. This team laughed together, cried together, prayed together and stood tall together over the course of the season. Our coaching staff couldn't be more proud of these young men. I hope Auburn fans feel the same way.

It's not just the fact that they went 13-0, won the Southeastern Conference championship and did everything they could to win a national championship, but it's the way they went about it.

A group like this one deserves a book about its perfect season. There will be other outstanding teams at Auburn, but there will never be another team or season exactly like the 2004 team. This team deserves a special place in Auburn history.

I hope you enjoy *An Inside Look at a Perfect Season: Tales from the Auburn 2004 Championship Season*, a collection of stories and memories for the Auburn family to cherish and share. I know I will always treasure all the people and the hard work and character it took to make this book possible.

War Eagle!

—Tommy Tuberville, Auburn head coach

Acknowledgments

First, I have to think God for the opportunity to write this book. My life has been blessed beyond measure by the open doors God has provided me along this incredible journey. Like so many other blessings on my path, I never saw this one coming.

Of course, I have to thank my loved ones, especially Karen, Colin, Taylor, Bo and Grace, who have to live with me through the writing process; also, my mom and dad, my mother, Michael and Casie (I got it right this time), Connor, Ryan, Logan, mom and dad Hulce, Lori, Greg and Sean, Ron, Dana, Louie and Zoe.

Special thanks goes to Mountaintop Community Church, our small group, Team 45, my high school and creative arts friends, Emily Dickinson, South City Theatre and all those people who make my life a better place to live.

Long overdue thanks to Jo Anne and Edd Johnson, my all-time favorite Auburn fans.

Professional gratitude to the many media outlets and beat writers covering Auburn football, especially Phillip Marshall of the *Huntsville Times* and Charles Goldberg of the *Birmingham News*. This book would not have been possible without the research found in the *Huntsville Times*, the *Birmingham News*, the *Birmingham Post-Herald*, the *Mobile Register*, the *Montgomery Advertiser*, the *Columbus Ledger-Enquirer*, the *Decatur Daily* and *Opelika-Auburn News*, as well as Auburnsports.com and AUtigers.com.

Personal and professional gratitude to Auburn coach Tommy Tuberville; his coaching staff, especially Joe Whitt for his time, kindness and fishin' hole; the Auburn players for sharing their time, stories and hearts; Jean Davis for her grace and generosity over the years; the media relations staff, particularly Meredith Jenkins and Kirk Sampson, for patiently and effectively holding my hand and leading me through this process; photographer Todd Van Emst; and David Housel, who opened so many doors for me at Auburn.

And, once again, my deepest thanks to my favorite scrum half and editor, Gina Sabbia, for her patience, understanding and enthusiasm throughout this journey.

INTRODUCTION

"Look at Us Now"

The irony proved to be as thick as the crowd of more than 5,000 eager football coaches attending the American Football Coaches Association in downtown Louisville, Kentucky, in early January. Coaches from all levels of high school and college football packed shoulder to shoulder in the Kentucky International Convention Center to hear Auburn coach Tommy Tuberville.

Just 14 months before, just nine miles away, just across the Ohio River, a private jet carrying an entourage led by former University President William Walker landed at the Clark County Airport in Jeffersonville, Indiana, to meet with Louisville coach Bobby Petrino about replacing Tuberville as Auburn's head coach.

And here Tuberville stood at the podium, the 2004 AFCA Division I-A Coach of the Year, to deliver a speech on the topic: "Perseverance in Coaching."

Ironic indeed. Appropriate for certain.

"It was a tough year," Tuberville told his audience, "but look at us now."

Take a good long look, because the 14 months between Tuberville's near exit and his stunning emergence as one of the nation's most recognized college football coaches and Auburn's extraordinary rise from enigmatic underachiever to national prominence combine to tell a tale too astonishing to believe if it weren't so true.

As Tuberville said so many times in the months between his imminent departure and the completion of a 13-0 season, "I had already put in my application to be a greeter at Wal-Mart."

Instead of pointing people to the discount clearance racks, Tuberville, along with his coaches and his senior leaders, spent the 2004 season pointing the way toward the top of the college football world.

In the end, Auburn had to share that peak with the Southern California Trojans, the official Bowl Championship Series national champions, but the Tigers remained undefeated, undaunted and unwavering in their claim to the title.

"Nobody can take that away from us," senior running back Carnell "Cadillac" Williams said. "We'll probably go down as the best team that ever played at Auburn. This team has just special coaches and special players. We try to do everything with class. We went to class and worked in the community and won games and had fun doing it."

CHAPTER 1

The Offseason: Starting Over

For all the glow surrounding Auburn's extraordinary 2004 season, the roots of Auburn's transformation are deeply and undeniably embedded in the controversy surrounding the ill-fated trip to hire Louisville coach Bobby Petrino and the days and weeks that followed. However, to fully understand those events and their impact, it's important to go back to the spring of 2003 when Auburn emerged as an early preseason contender for the national championship.

Led by linebackers Karlos Dansby and Dontarrious Thomas and running backs Ronnie Brown and Carnell Williams, the Tigers returned 16 starters and a bounty of reasons to support those championship predictions. In April 2003, when *Lindy's Southeastern Football* interviewed Tuberville for a season preview story, coach Tommy Tuberville and his players did nothing to discourage the high expectations surrounding the program.

In a more telling moment during the same interview session, Tuberville took stock of the situation, considered the direction of his program and hinted his team might still be another year away from making a national run.

"I think we can be pretty good this year," Tuberville said of the 2003 team, "but I think we could be even better next year."

Despite his assessment and his concerns, Auburn entered the season as a No. 1 pick in two polls and the consensus choice to win the SEC. When the Tigers opened with embarrassing losses to USC and Georgia Tech and stumbled to an 8-5 finish, Tuberville came dangerously close to losing his job in a controversial fiasco that left a scar and made Auburn tougher in the long run.

MISGUIDED MISSION

The heat began to rise under Tuberville's seat following the 17-3 loss to underdog Georgia Tech. As the former dean of engineering at Auburn, losing to Tech left university president William Walker both embarrassed and angry enough to rip into athletic director David Housel outside the athletic director's box at Tech's Grant Field.

As the season wore on and high expectations turned to talk of Tuberville's tenuous job security, Walker started making his move. When Auburn lost 26-7 at Georgia on November 15, 2003, Walker made his decision and secretly hired a Chicago executive search firm owned by John Mengelt, a former Auburn basketball standout, to assist with the search for a new coach.

Walker centered his search on Petrino, who spent the 2002 season at Auburn as Tuberville's offensive coordinator before taking over as Louisville's head coach. On November 20, two days before Auburn's home game with Alabama, Walker defied Housel's advice and secured a private jet owned by Colonial Bank, where Auburn's most prominent booster, Robert E. "Bobby" Lowder is the chairman and CEO.

Walker flew to southern Indiana, along with Housel and two members of the Board of Trustees, president pro tempore Earlon McWhorter and former Auburn wide receiver Byron Franklin. Housel told Walker the trip was a bad idea, especially the timing of a trip just two days before the Iron Bowl. Housel also reminded Walker that universities and presidents make a common practice of asking for permission to interview candidates. When Walker refused his counsel, Housel decided he had to make the trip to keep close tabs on the situation.

WALKING THROUGH THE FIRE

In the days leading up to the Alabama game, Tuberville quickly realized something wasn't right. Alabama Governor Bob Riley even called Tuberville to find out what Tuberville knew. When Tuberville asked Housel if he had already been fired and replaced by Petrino, Housel denied any knowledge of a decision. At the same time, Petrino had already begun talking to possible assistant coaches about bringing them to Auburn.

"Coaches know," Tuberville said. "I knew. I couldn't get anybody to talk to me. Couldn't get any answers."

The players knew, too, and the coaches did what they could to keep them focused on the most important game of the season.

"We were playing Alabama during this whole big charade and our players were able to focus on it because of [team chaplain] Chette Williams and our coaches talking to them, telling them 'this isn't about us' and reminding them it is about team,'" Tuberville said. "We told them, 'Don't win for us. Win for yourselves, for each other. This is the biggest game of the year. This is our championship.'"

The Tigers won that game 28-23, but Walker refused to change his mind. His plan was to vacation in Texas, let the glow of the Alabama win fade and then return to officially fire Tuberville and hire Petrino. News, even supposed clandestine news, tends to travel fast across the Auburn camp when it is pushed by the winds of controversy. Three days after the Alabama game, newspaper reporters in Louisville and Montgomery started investigating why a jet owned by Colonial Bank, where Lowder is the president and chief executive officer, landed at the Clark County Airport. It didn't take long to add one and one together and come up with a long list of questions and answers about who knew what and when. Before long, the incident became known as "Jetgate" and brought a barrage of criticism down on the university, particularly Walker.

Auburn fans responded with a hurricane of criticism for Walker, Housel and the guilty trustees. Walker, clearly embarrassed about getting caught in the act, initially reacted by issuing contradictory statements on consecutive days. Finally, he relented under pressure from Riley and "asked" Tuberville to remain.

Tuberville, in an emotional session with the media following a private meeting with Walker, choked back tears as he announced his deci-

After a disappointing 2003 season the Tigers
rallied around coach Tommy Tuberville.
Photo by Todd J. Van Emst

sion to remain at Auburn. Despite his anger and his lack of trust in Walker and Housel, Tuberville offered his public forgiveness. Walker and Housel were eventually forced out of their jobs by Riley and new interim president Ed Richardson. Walker was fired, Housel chose to retire, and Tuberville and his team started over.

"It would have been pretty easy to point fingers, blame people and walk out with a pretty big check," Tuberville said. Instead, Tuberville told his staff, "If these kids are ever going to learn anything from us, they are going to learn how to handle adversity. We're not going to hold grudges. We're not going to talk about the past. We're going to talk about the future. We don't want this to linger."

Tuberville added, "In 30 years of coaching, I've never seen anything like the way this team has rallied around each other. We went through some tough times when I knew I wasn't going to come back. But two of the reasons I did come back after the whole 'Jetgate' deal was that the players stayed behind us 110 percent and the fans did as well.

"These players grew up a lot in those two weeks. I think they learned a lot from the situation I was in about how to do things, how not to do things and how to focus on what's important."

In the process, Tuberville's public resolve also set the wheels of a turnaround season in four-wheel motion.

"Everybody else thought he was gone, but we saw something different," said Tommy "T.J." Jackson, a junior starter at noseguard. "We never saw him give up or get mad. He was so debonair about it. Most guys would have cracked up under that pressure, but he handled it and put us first, just like we were his own kids. That's why we love him. That's why we followed him."

Williams said, "It started last year with Coach Tub. The things he went through, the way he handled that whole situation, we saw that and knew he was special. We rallied around that."

ONE MORE YEAR

In a year defined by so many decisive turning points, the next chapter came in early January when three star players and team leaders, running backs Brown and Williams and cornerback Carlos Rogers, all decided to pass up the NFL draft and return for their senior seasons— even if it meant Williams and Brown would have to share the ball and the spotlight and Rogers would spend his senior season wondering if quarterbacks would ever throw his way. None of the three could know for certain that their decisions would lead to a 13-0 season and individual honors.

"I knew it could happen because of the type of people we are," Williams said. "We're more about team, more about winning. But I never thought it would work out like it did, with both of us doing real well. It's sweet."

FLYING BENEATH THE RADAR

The next turning point came when Tuberville sat down with his offensive coaches and decided to bring in a new offensive coordinator. When Petrino left after the 2002 season Tuberville wanted to keep his offensive scheme intact and promoted offensive line coach Hugh Nall to coordinate the offense and brought in Steve Ensminger to coach the quarterbacks and help call the plays. While the Tigers showed marked improvement in their final two games of the season, it proved to be an awkward situation Tuberville had to fix.

"Hugh and I sat down and discussed the situation and came to the conclusion that we were going to have to bring someone else in here," Tuberville said. "He agreed that we needed someone who could come in with the ability to run and throw the ball with the personnel we had."

That someone proved to be veteran assistant Al Borges, who worked closely with Nall and the offensive staff to install a version of the West Coast offense designed to make the best possible use of Williams, Brown and Campbell. Through a nondescript offseason in which the defense attempted to replace Dansby and Thomas and two other starters among the front seven and some awkward initial steps in a new offense, the Tigers did nothing to convince anyone—including themselves—they should be picked to finish any higher than 15th nationally and second in the SEC West.

SUMMER SCHOOL

In fact, the workouts that followed spring practice initially created more doubt than confidence. Football coaches like to insist seasons are often won from January to July when players are lifting, running, stretching and building themselves into better football players. It's during that time when players are expected to grow in strength, size, speed and maturity.

If that's truly the case, the first six months of 2004 did little to convince head strength and conditioning coach Kevin Yoxall that Auburn's season would be anything special.

"I've had other winter and spring training periods where it went better from the standpoint of testing and numbers in the weight room," Yoxall said. "We didn't have a lot of colossal numbers in our testing."

In fact, at times the spring was both disappointing and frustrating for Yoxall. Under new NCAA rules that came into place in the spring of 2004, teams were no longer allowed to hold mandatory workouts every week from January 1 to May 31. Instead, strength and conditioning coaches were forced to choose eight "discretionary" weeks in which players were not required to report for daily workouts.

Considering the history of his players, Yoxall hoped, and even expected, a strong turnout when Auburn entered the longest fraction of its discretionary period after spring football.

"We had a big meeting, before finals, where I told them, 'Here's the deal: your discretionary time is about to start. If you show up, you know I'm going to work your butt off, so here are the times when we're available,'" Yoxall said. "Let's be honest. Most of these kids are 18 to 21 years old, and I didn't have a lot of them show up. I was really kind of disappointed."

When the spring turned to summer, Yoxall decided it was time to sit down with each player individually both to discuss their goals and needs and to tell them how he felt about their spring workout attendance.

"I laid it out there," Yoxall said. "I told them how they should have been in here, how they should have been training. At that point, I've got to tell you I was very concerned, because I felt like we were behind where we needed to be. But once we got into summer, things really began to click."

For all the credit given the head coach and assistant coaches, it's possible that in most programs, the strength and conditioning coaches actually spend more time with the players. That's certainly true with Auburn players and Yoxall and his staff.

Yet, while strength and conditioning coaches can oversee summer workouts, no member of the coaching staff can get involved in any way when the players take to the practice fields when quarterbacks, receivers and backs do their throwing, catching and covering on their own.

It's a summer rite that rarely involves non-skill players, but that changed last summer when players from all positions found themselves taking part in group and individual drills.

"This summer it was every position," Yoxall said. "Offensive line. Defensive line. They were out there in some sort of highly organized fashion at least three nights a week, putting themselves through position skill drills, running plays, being a lot more organized than I'd ever seen before. A lot of nights they were here long after I had gone, and me and my guys and the trainers are usually the last ones out of the building.

"I think the kids sensed what all of us coaches, myself included, went through last year and I know that was probably on their minds as well. They might have felt they needed to take more ownership in this thing than they had in the past."

Under the heat and pressure of a searing southern summer, the Tigers took major steps toward becoming a true team with the older, established players pointing the way and younger players following their lead.

"I think a lot of it started during summer workouts," said defensive end Doug Langenfeld, a senior starter in 2004. "The coaches can't be out there with us, pushing us, but we had a bunch of guys out there running in the heat of the afternoon. At that point it would have been easy to say, 'Man, I don't want to run today, it's too hot,' but we had a lot of leaders out there pushing guys to run, even if we had to help a guy cross the line and finish his run."

Jackson added, "Summer workouts are supposed to be 'volunteer,' but you know what 'volunteer' means. It's hot, it's tough and you see what you have as a team. We had a lot of guys pushing and pulling each other through those workouts, saying we're not going to quit because we really do want to become something, we really do want to be a championship team.

"That's when I knew that no matter what happened this year we were going to have each other's backs, that we were going to stick together. I really think that was the whole turning point for this team, when we really learned to lean on each other."

PLAY TIME

The players also found themselves spending more time together, whether it was daily summer gatherings at local pools, meals, parties, marathon video game competitions or volunteering to bail hay or build fences at Storybrook Farms, a non-profit therapeutic horseback riding facility for children in Opelika.

"We started doing a lot of things together," said receiver Courtney Taylor, a sophomore starter. "There was a Saturday when we were off for some reason and all of us got together to play softball against some fraternity boys. It was so hilarious. You wouldn't believe how many guys on this team cannot play a lick of softball. You would think athletes would be able to do anything, but they can't swing, they can't catch, they can't throw.

"But that's one time that sticks out as some of the most fun I've ever had. That's when I really came to accept Auburn as home. You come here and live with guys you don't even know, but they become your best friends."

The result isn't nearly as memorable as the day itself.

"I don't even know if we won," Taylor said. "We just played for like three or four hours. We were just having fun. It's like playing football when you're kids and you play so long you lose track."

Those same big kids also spent an entire day losing track of time and money shooting paintball at each other on a local farm.

"This summer a bunch of us got together and went out and played paintball," Taylor said. "I'm talking something like 40 guys and it got real competitive. Some of the guys on this team cheat so bad. They act like they're out of the game and they'll turn around and shoot you.

"We were out there all day and every time we'd finish a game we'd say, 'Let's play another game.' We were out there so long we were broke by the time we got back, but it was worth it."

BETTER LIVING THROUGH CHEMISTRY

Around that same time, the team's spiritual identity also experienced a dynamic development, with the weekly team Bible study directed by Chette Williams attracting as many as 60-70 players at a time.

"We would discuss the Bible, pray for each other, share, preach, cry, confess," Chette Williams said. "It really took off. That was about the same time T.J. was going through a tough situation and T.J. got up and shared his faith in adversity. Some of the kids got baptized. People talk about togetherness and love . . . you just saw it happening there.

"That started in the winter and grew through the spring, but it really took off in July and I just started seeing guys bonding in an unbelievable way. They took that same chemistry into the season."

They also took their share of questions into a season of uncertainty—questions that could only be answered on the field.

CHAPTER 2

Louisiana-Monroe: Far from Perfect

Louisiana-Monroe? The season opener had very little do with Louisiana-Monroe and everything to do with Auburn. After defeating Louisiana-Monroe 73-7 in 2002, the Tigers weren't concerned with the Indians. Instead, 17th-ranked Auburn's true opponent in its 2004 season opener would be itself.

How would the offense work under new coordinator Al Borges after struggling throughout most of the 2003 season? How would the defense play with four new starters among its front seven and uncertainty at the cornerback spot opposite cornerback Carlos Rogers? How would the Tigers open the season after losing consecutive openers to Southern Cal?

ULM was obviously no USC, but in a 31-0 victory over the Indians Auburn dropped plenty of hints of being a new breed of Tigers.

"It was a good start," coach Tommy Tuberville said. "There are a lot of things we need to work on, but that's what the first game is for."

JUST A HINT

The offense looked like a work in progress, but at least the passing game got off to a good start. After struggling with productivity and consistency throughout the 2003 season, the revamped passing game allowed senior quarterback Jason Campbell to complete 11 of 18 passes for 110 yards with two touchdowns, but he also lost a fumble and threw an interception. The one-sided nature of the game also allowed redshirt freshman quarterback Brandon Cox to see some much-needed playing time. In all, eight receivers caught at least one pass.

The Tigers scored on their first three possessions, but they weren't fooling themselves into thinking they had found all their answers.

"We kind of got off to a slow start, but it's our first ballgame in a new offense," senior tailback Carnell Williams said. "We're looking pretty good . . . . There's still a lot more you're going to see. We're not going to show everything at this stage."

The defense also did its part, recording a shutout and playing plenty of second- and third-team reserves in the second half. Not all of the news was positive, though. ULM quarterback Steve Jyles completed his first 11 passes, the Indians ran for 140 yards and the Tigers played without starting cornerback Montae Pitts, who missed the game due to a suspension for violating team policy.

"Defensively, we ran around well," Tuberville said. "The first-team defense looked really good. The second team gave up some plays, but that's going to happen. It was a good learning experience for all of them."

MOVING ON

So what did Auburn learn from this opener? For openers, the Tigers played 73 players, including 21 players who saw their first action as Tigers and six true freshmen. Add a shutout from the defense and some progress from the offense, and the Tigers at least made the opener a worthwhile experience.

"We went to work, got it done," Tuberville said. "Now we've got to get better."

At least the Tigers had the schedule working in their favor. As the Tigers flipped the page on Louisiana-Monroe and turned their attention toward Mississippi State, they could look into the not-so-distant future and see some interesting possibilities.

"We've got a good schedule this year," offensive line coach Hugh Nall said. "That's the way you'd like it every year—start with a team that you should beat, iron out some problems, or find out some problems, and work on a few things. Then you start working your way up. Our schedule is perfect for that."

Perfect? That wasn't a word anyone associated with Auburn at that point. Not even the Tigers themselves would dare to think of such a thing, let alone speak it.

"We have Mississippi State coming up," senior strong safety Junior Rosegreen said, "and when you are in the SEC, every game is big."

CHAPTER 3

The Offense: "Brains Before Beauty"

When someone suggested to Al Borges midway through the 2004 season that he had emerged as one of the nation's hottest offensive coordinators, Borges had to laugh.

"You mean hot like a great-looking guy?" Borges said.

Well, OK, not that kind of hot. After all, the bald, bulbous Borges isn't exactly Brad Pitt. What he is is an accomplished football coach who arrived at Auburn in February and helped transform an underachieving Auburn offense into a multidimensional machine capable of running, passing, controlling the clock and scoring.

With Borges running the show, calling the plays and making the best use of Auburn's personnel, the Tigers improved from eighth in the SEC in scoring in 2003 to first in the conference in 2004, with 32.1 points per game. The Tigers also improved from sixth in total offense to second, with 420.7 yards per game. Most important, the offense carried its share of the load throughout a 13-0 season.

Not bad for a coach who wasn't exactly the first choice of fans and critics when he was hired over up-and-comers such as Miami of Ohio's Shane Montgomery or Toledo's Rob Spence, young coordinators running the wide-open shotgun spread offenses that have become so trendy in recent years.

While fans on message boards and certain sports radio hosts ripped Auburn coach Tommy Tuberville for bringing in an unknown coach from that noted football factory Indiana, people in the coaching business immediately saw it as a great hire, especially those who coached with or against Borges on the West Coast, where he is respected as both a coordinator and a quarterback mentor after coaching for eight conference champions, helping UCLA win 20 consecutive games in 1997-98, coaching a Heisman finalist in UCLA quarterback Cade McNown and finishing as a finalist for the Frank Broyles Assistant Coach of the Year Award in 1997 and 1998.

"If you just looked at what I'd done lately, you weren't going to hire me," Borges said. "But if you look at the totality of my resume, I was a fabulous candidate. I say that not arrogantly but truthfully. I know the other guys who interviewed for this job, and none of them were even close, but I wasn't the sexiest candidate."

Alabama secondary coach Chris Ball, who coached against Borges at Washington State, told the *Birmingham News*, "People back here probably hadn't even heard of him a whole lot. I knew what he brought to the table. I knew Coach Tuberville made a really good hire."

STARTING OVER

Borges understood his lack of name recognition in the South and knew the only way he could prove himself was to get the job done on game days. In the meantime, he helped disarm some of the negative talk with his candid approach in media interviews and his self-deprecating humor on radio call-in shows.

"I'm a guy who likes to enjoy life, and football is a big part of my life," Borges said. "I don't like the sterile image that some coaches portray. That's just not my personality."

That personality helped when he arrived as Auburn's fourth offensive coordinator in four years to find a skeptical group of offensive players who didn't know Borges from Knute Rockne. After quarterback Jason Campbell saw an *ESPN Classic* replay of UCLA's 49-45 victory over Miami in 1998 he asked Borges if he had ever seen the game. Borges had to tell him he was UCLA's offensive coordinator that day.

"I had no idea who he was," Campbell said. "When I heard about it, I was just thinking, 'Here we go again. Time to start over.'"

When wide receiver Ben Obomanu was first introduced to Borges, "I was just watching him," Obomanu said. "I was thinking, 'This guy reminds me of somebody'—it just took me a while to think of who it was."

Turns out it was Rodney Dangerfield, the late comedian known for his starring roles in *Caddyshack* and *Back to School* and his ability to find humor in his misfortune.

Funny thing is, Borges's own career had fallen into misfortune after a wrong turn somewhere between Los Angeles and Berkeley. After climbing the ladder from coaching in the California high school ranks to jobs as a graduate assistant at the University of California and full-time jobs at Diablo Valley College, the USFL's Oakland Invaders, Portland State, Boise State, Oregon and UCLA, Borges returned to Cal as the team's offensive coordinator in 2001. The Bears went 1-10 and Borges was fired along with head coach Tom Holmoe and the rest of the staff.

"It blew up in my face," Borges said. "It was the biggest mistake I ever made, not because it was Cal. I love Cal. But because when I got there everything went wrong—players getting injured, turning up ineligible, problem after problem after problem. It got to where I hated to go into work every day because something bad was going to happen."

Borges started over and spent two years at Indiana before Tuberville came calling, looking for a veteran coach who could find a way to make good use of Auburn's personnel instead of re-vamping the entire offense in favor of his own system. Tuberville told Borges he had to adopt Auburn's existing terminology. Then he stepped back and let Borges go to work.

"The first thing about Tommy is that he gives full autonomy to the coordinators," Borges said. "I work best that way. You pretty much have carte blanche to do what you think it takes to move the ball, that's No. 1. No. 2 is he is a really, really good game manager, especially through some bad times, which fortunately, we haven't seen much of this year. When I got here, I know they went through some times, but he managed to keep the team together."

FITTING IN

Those tough times led Tuberville to overhaul his coaching staff following the 2003 season, with offensive line coach Hugh Nall no longer coordinating the offense and assistant coach Steve Ensminger no longer helping Nall with the play calling and switching from coaching the quarterbacks to the tight ends.

Instead of making life difficult for the new offensive coordinator, Nall and Ensminger made sure Borges knew he was welcome. For his part, Borges went out of his way to make sure the returning coaches would have his ear and his respect.

"Al is such a great guy," Nall said. "There's not a better guy in the world that we could have hired to make this work and the chemistry work. He's really a class act."

OPENING THE LINES OF COMMUNICATION

Convincing the players took a little more time, especially Campbell. For starters, Campbell didn't have much to say, and when he did, Borges often struggled to understand his southern accent and low voice.

"At first I didn't talk much," Campbell said. "He said, 'Do you ever say anything?' I said, 'Yeah, but I've just got to feel you out first.'"

The more time they spent together, they more they began to communicate. The more they communicated, the more Campbell took down his guard and relaxed. Before long, they were laughing and joking, and players were kidding Campbell, calling Borges his "daddy."

Most important, Borges slowly but surely worked to shape and build Campbell's self-confidence, mechanics and knowledge of the offense.

"You want to be on the same page with the coordinator," Campbell said. "You want to think alike. The main thing he and I had that was better than the past, we just communicated more."

"A CHANCE TO BE PRETTY GOOD"

Once Borges had Campbell's confidence and attention, he also had to earn the respect of running backs Carnell Williams and Ronnie Brown, both of whom passed up a chance to enter the NFL Draft and return for their senior seasons with hopes of sharing the ball, only to learn that Borges would be running his own version of the West Coast offense.

*The offensive scheme and play-calling of offensive coordinator Al
Borges played a significant role in Auburn's success.*
Photo by Todd J. Van Emst

"When I heard 'West Coast offense,' I thought we were going to throw it 60 times a game, and I'd never the see the ball again," Williams said.

Instead, Borges had to convince his two best players that the West Coast offense was built around running the ball effectively to set up play-action passing and more passes to the backs. His plan was to use them both in multiple roles, with Brown playing some at fullback and splitting out as a receiver so he and Williams could play together at the same time.

"I had to do a little selling to Cadillac [Williams] and Ronnie," Borges said. "I told them the good news was that we were keeping most of the old running plays. The better news is that they'd see more running lanes and get a chance to catch some out of the backfield."

By the end of spring practice, due in large part to Borges's willingness to adapt to Auburn's terminology, the players were convinced.

"It only took about two weeks for us to get the hang of this offense in spring practice, and then suddenly I'm looking around and everybody is smiling," Campbell said. "I'm happy, Carnell and Ronnie are happy, everybody is happy. We started thinking, 'Man, we've got a chance to be pretty good.'"

WHAT'S NEXT?

Still, no one knew for certain until the season started. Game by game, the offense improved and adjusted to every new scheme and strategy it saw. When opponents made an obvious commitment to stopping Williams and Brown, Campbell and an improved group of receivers learned to make them pay with the passing game. In the process, Auburn became the balanced team it had wanted to be for so long and developed into an effective third-down team, converting 45.9 percent of its third downs into first downs. Even better, the Tigers became a dangerous offensive team capable of striking lightning with a big play—whether it was Campbell going deep or a well-timed trick play.

"That goes a long way with the players," wide receiver Courtney Taylor said. "We know this guy is going to put the time in to be here all day and all night, to put us in the best position. You've got to love him. We never take a step back. It's just exciting to see what this guy is going to come up with next. You never know what's next."

WHIP SMART

Ask Borges about his contribution to Auburn's success in 2004, and he'll be more likely to admit he's a hot-looking guy. He'd rather tell you about the players, the other coaches and one of the nation's top defenses.

"In my heart of hearts, I would love to think I'd made this much difference. I have not," Borges said. "I have a quarterback who had been here three years who was ready to be a good player. I've got two NFL running backs who when they leave here are going to play as long as they can stay healthy."

Besides, Borges added, "There are no geniuses in coaching. It's just that some guys are more innovative than other guys and are willing to try more things than other guys. You can be smart as a whip and not look very smart."

SMART GUY

By the end of the 2004 season, Borges looked pretty smart—especially for a guy who wasn't the sexiest hire.

"I acquired more brain cells, and my intellect went up 60 to 70 points when I got Jason Campbell, Ronnie Brown and Carnell Williams," Borges said. "It's just incredible how that can happen.

"Seriously, what any offensive coach is looking for is some weapons, guys who can score touchdowns so that you can gear your plan to getting them the ball."

All that—and a chance to coach in big games for big stakes in front of big crowds.

"I came here it because I thought Auburn could win and win now," Borges said. "I thought I'd rather come into a supposedly high-risk situation with athletic players in a fabulous conference with a chance to win than being in a continuous rebuilding situation."

IT'S A SOUTHERN THING

Borges admitted he still has a lot to learn about living in Alabama, and he still won't touch grits, but it didn't take long for him to learn the difference between West Coast football and college football in the South.

"It didn't happen like this anywhere I'd ever been before," Borges said. "Our players feed on the enthusiasm of the fans. Everywhere I've been, you get off the bus, go in the locker room sit there and kind of wait around a little bit, put on your stuff, go out for warmups, kick it off and play.

"Here, when you step off the bus—as much or more away from home as at home—there are 20,000 screaming fans that you have to walk through. They can't wait to see you play. When our kids get to the locker room, they are still charged up."

CHAPTER 4

Mississippi State: One at a Time

There's a reason why coaches use the same old clichés time and time again. They work. So when a coach talks about "taking it one game at a time," he's usually trying to make a valid point.

Check any team that remains successful over the course of an entire season, and you'll find a team that really does take it "one game at a time" instead of getting caught up in looking ahead. They keep their heads on straight, make the most of that week's game and take care of the task at hand before moving on.

Alabama did it in 1992. Auburn did it in 1993. Tennessee did it in 1998. Oklahoma did it in 2000. All four teams finished undefeated. Add Auburn's 2004 team to the list.

That special trait was evident early on in the 2004 season, starting with the second game of the season. If Auburn was looking past Mississippi State, it sure didn't show on the second Saturday in September in Starkville, Mississippi.

With quarterback Jason Campbell throwing three touchdown passes, including two to wide receiver Anthony Mix, the 18th-ranked Tigers wasted little time in building a 14-0 lead, led 21-0 at halftime and ran away for a 43-14 victory over the Bulldogs.

Auburn's defense didn't allow the Bulldogs to advance inside its 30-yard line in the first half, and Mississippi State's two scores didn't come until the game's final 83 seconds, against Auburn's second- and third-team defenders.

"We played with a lot of intensity, and a lot better than we did last week," Auburn coach Tommy Tuberville said. "We wanted to come out and control the line of scrimmage, and we did that. We improved, running the football, and we wanted to control the clock.

"Defensively, we made a lot of big plays, and the first team put up a shutout until we put in our second team."

OUTMANNED, OVERMATCHED

Even first-year Mississippi State coach Sylvester Croom had to step back and admit he had just seen a better team take control of the game and not let up until the outcome was well in hand.

"They beat us in about every way they could," Croom said. "It doesn't take a genius to figure out what they did. They beat us on the line of scrimmage."

Croom's biggest concern during the week before the outcome had been the running game, with good reason. Ronnie Brown rushed for 147 yards on 15 carries while Carnell Williams finished with 123 yards and two touchdowns on 19 attempts.

"I knew that they were NFL-quality backs," Croom said. "I looked at them for a couple of years when I was at Green Bay. You will see them playing on Sunday next year. I knew going into the game what we would be facing."

TAKING AIM

Auburn also entered the game knowing it would face the temptation to look ahead and focus on the next game against defending national champion LSU. Auburn not only dominated the Bulldogs but managed to put thoughts of LSU away until it was safe to look forward.

"We've been trying hard for the past two weeks not to let them look ahead," Tuberville said. "With the intensity they played with today, it looked like they were focused on this game."

"LSU is always in the back of your mind," offensive tackle Marcus McNeil said. "They're the national champions and they have a real big bull's-eye on their chest. Everybody wants a piece of them."

Nobody wanted a bigger piece than Auburn. With LSU coming to town ranked fifth in the nation and Auburn moving up to No. 14, the stage was set for a nationally televised showdown that would go a long way toward defining Auburn's heart and soul.

"We are going to take it to another level," strong safety Junior Rosegreen said. "We went down there last year and they beat us to death [31-7].

"We feel like we owe them. They are going to come in ready to play. We're going to be ready to play. It's going to be a great game."

CHAPTER 5

The Defense: Too Small, Too Unknown ... Too Tough

Before star linebackers Karlos Dansby and Dontarrious Thomas left Auburn to begin their NFL careers in the spring of 2004, they presented their former teammates with a prediction that defied the expectations for a defense surrounded by questions and concerns.

With only three returning starters among the front seven, several unproven young players in key roles and a secondary that still had a lot to prove, the Tigers appeared to be one of the weak links in Auburn's chain entering spring practice.

Dansby and Thomas, however, didn't see it that way. They saw beyond the surface, past returning starters and experience, to a quality that's difficult for outsiders to understand.

Strong safety Junior Rosegreen recalled Dansby and Thomas telling him, "Y'all are going to be way better than us. Last year we had a lot of Is and there's not an I in team. Y'all got a team. Y'all are faster than we were. You need to take it one game at a time and one play at a time, and all this is going to be special year for y'all."

That was easy to say in the spring, but not so easy to see, even for some of the players themselves. Between the loss of Dansby and Thomas and linemen Reggie Torbor and Spencer Johnson to the NFL, as well as starting tackle DeMarco McNeil, some of the younger players looked around and wondered where the defense stood.

"The second all those guys left, everybody started talking about 'Oh man, we're going to replace Karlos and Dontarrious and all those guys,'" senior defensive end Bret Eddins said. "A lot of guys on defense kind of took it hard in the spring but the older players knew the guys who were coming up were talented. They just didn't have the age and the experience. We also knew with time and game experience they were going to be great. But all those guys came along a lot faster than I ever thought they would."

ALL THE RIGHT MOVES

The came along so fast that the Tigers finished the 2004 season as the nation's leading scoring defense, allowing only 11.3 points per game and playing a huge role in Auburn's 13-0 finish. The Tigers also finished fifth in the nation in total defense, allowing just 277.62 yards per game, and 12th in rushing defense, allowing only 104.2 yards per game and just four rushing touchdowns.

"I don't want to say that it has been a huge surprise, because I've always had a lot of confidence in our players," said defensive coordinator Gene Chizik, who left Auburn in January 2005 to take the same position at the University of Texas. "We went through a lot of ups and downs in two-a-days and spring practice, but spring practice was a time where we had to try and identify where our problems were."

Auburn actually opened spring practice with more questions than answers. Outside of cornerback Carlos Rogers, linebacker Travis Williams, Rosegreen and Eddins, the suspects outnumbered the prospects. Who would replace Thomas at middle linebacker? Who would play the corner opposite Rogers? Who would step up to become dependable players on the line? Would Auburn's small linebackers be able to hold up against the run?

"Usually in the spring, it's the offense that's behind the defense," Auburn coach Tommy Tuberville said. "But we couldn't get our offense stopped."

Over the course of the spring, Chizik and the defensive coaching staff—line coaches Terry Price and Don Dunn and linebackers coach Joe Whitt—implemented several changes that turned out to be decisive

*Auburn's "no-name" defense, led by defensive coordinator Gene
Chizik, exceeded expectations in 2004.*
Photo by Todd J. Van Emst

steps for the defense. The coaches moved Travis Williams from the outside to the middle, senior Jay Ratliff moved from defensive end to tackle, Karibi Dede moved from safety to backup linebacker and Quentin
Groves, who came to Auburn as a defensive end before moving to linebacker during his redshirt year in 2003, moved back to defensive end.
During the same period, several young players stepped up and showed
the potential to be dependable full-time players, including nose guard

Tommy Jackson and outside linebacker Antarrious Williams, who briefly moved to free safety in the spring before moving back to linebacker. Sophomore end Stanley McClover, a sophomore who sat out the 2003 season as a partial qualifier, stood out as one of the brightest surprises of the spring.

When concerns about the defense found their way into print and regular discussions of Auburn football, it only served to make the players more determined to prove their critics wrong.

"We put a chip on our shoulders because everybody said that we 'can't,'" Rosegreen said. "'Can't' should never be in a man's vocabulary. We just feel like whoever said 'We can't,' doesn't really know us, and we wanted to show them that we can."

Travis Williams added, "We knew that we had talent. We knew we had to prove it to the doubters. And we set out to prove it from the first game."

SOMETHING LEFT TO PROVE

The Tigers faced unexpected adversity before they could ever play a game when they lost cornerback David Irons, a projected starter, to a season-ending knee injury in preseason practice. Then the cornerback who eventually earned the starting job, Montavis Pitts, had to sit out the first game because of a suspension for violating team rules. With Rogers playing through a nagging knee injury and backup cornerback Courtney Denson transferring to South Florida so he could play quarterback, the Tigers had a lot of concerns to address.

Even though the Tigers held Louisiana-Monroe scoreless in the opener, they knew they still had a lot to prove once the SEC opened the next week at Mississippi State.

The Tigers got a better idea in a 43-14 victory at Mississippi State, with second- and third-teamers allowing both scores in the final 1:23 of the game, but it wasn't until the LSU game that the Tigers started to believe in themselves and see what Dansby and Thomas knew all along.

OFFERING THE PROOF

After giving up six quick points against LSU and allowing nine points in the first half, the Auburn defense found its defining moment in the second half as it shut down LSU time and time again and allowed the offense every opportunity to score 10 points and win the game. "Back in the spring when we beat up on the offense, I thought we had a chance to be a real good defense," Rogers said, "but I didn't really know how it would play out once the game started.

"But in the LSU game I really felt like we all pulled together and united together as a unit and kept out focus and composure throughout all the ups and downs. At that point, I didn't know if we were going to win the SEC championship or not, but I knew we had a good enough defense to win it."

A WORK IN PROGRESS

Auburn's defensive progress was no accident. Chizik, who arrived from Central Florida in 2002 to replace John Lovett, expected it would take three years for everyone to get on the same page. He bought into Tuberville's defensive philosophy of favoring speed over size and saw that plan come to fruition in 2004. The Tigers weren't very big, but they proved to be fast, physical and tough with two starting 210-pound linebackers in Travis Williams and Antarrious Williams and two undersized ends, McGlover and Groves, playing situational roles off the bench and leading the team with 7.5 tackles each.

"Typically, your third year is really the year that is the break-out year for you as far as everybody being on the same page," Chizik said late in the 2004 season. "The execution of the defense is generally better. Even though a lot of our guys had not had a lot of starts prior to the beginning of the year, they have all been a product of the system."

Chizik also did his part, developing into one of the nation's better defensive coordinators in his three seasons at Auburn and earning the Frank Broyles Award, presented annually to the nation's top major college football assistant coach.

"Coach Lovett maybe didn't gel with the defensive backs and some of the older guys on the team as well as Coach Chizik has been able to," Eddins said. "It seems like everybody from front to back understands the defensive concept and what the coaches are trying to do. I doubt many guys did in the previous defense."

Offensive coordinator Al Borges saw that early in his first season at Auburn. "He does such a good job getting them lined up right," Borges said of Chizik. "When people beat us defensively, it's generally because somebody jumps over top of us, makes some miraculous play like [Alabama] did at the end of the game. We just don't make many errors on defense."

That became more and more evident as the season wore on and the defense grew in confidence. Even though quarterback Jason Campbell and the offense stood in the spotlight after an impressive 34-10 win at Tennessee on October 2, the defense did more than its share by forcing six turnovers, including four interceptions by Rosegreen.

"We were looking for continuity, and the schedule allowed us defensively to gain that continuity and to get better as the season progressed as a group," Chizik said. "On top of that, the guys got used to playing with each other and believing in each other."

That unity and confidence proved to be key character traits for a defense with few star players and an abundance of playmakers. Aside from Rogers, who went on to win the Thorpe Award as the nation's top defensive back, individual honors came few and far between for the Auburn defense.

NO NAMES? NO PROBLEM

Instead of bowing up at the term "no-name defense," the Tigers decided to embrace it as both a badge of honor and an attitude.

"Coach Dunn and Coach Price started calling us 'the replacements' back in the spring," Eddins said. "We joked about it a lot but we took it to heart when people said we weren't going to be that good this year."

"There were a lot of questions, as far as how good our defense was going to be, [because] we lost this person and that person," Travis Williams said. "This year we played as a team, and by playing as a team, we had more All-Americans, more All-SEC players. If you play as a team, good things will happen."

Players on the 2004 defense are quick to admit the 2003 defense had too many players trying to do their own thing, even if it didn't fit into the defensive scheme. For example, instead of controlling a gap so the linebacker could make the play, a defensive lineman might try to make the play himself and cause more harm than good, missing the tackle and getting in the linebacker's way.

"Last year a lot of people were out of position, trying to make plays they weren't supposed to make," Rogers said. "If we had a blitz called, they wanted to make the play and not take the back out or drag the lineman for somebody else to come free.

"This year we were just being smarter. You stay on your keys and don't try to be a hero. That's why we were a no-name defense. Everybody was out there making plays."

'OUR DEFENSE, WOW'

Whether it was holding Georgia to six points, making two critical stops inside the 10-yard line against Alabama, bouncing back from a poor third-quarter performance to finish strong in the SEC championship game against Tennessee or making a decisive goal-line stand in the Sugar Bowl against Virginia Tech, the Tigers made a habit of making plays throughout the season on the way to an SEC championship and an undefeated season.

"Our defense, wow," Auburn running back Carnell Williams said after the Sugar Bowl victory. "I've been reading a lot of stuff where they said we weren't playing for a national championship because our defense didn't have good-looking athletes on defense, we had a small defense, an undersized defense. I'd take our defense over anybody in the country."

CHAPTER 6

LSU:
As the Season Turns

While Auburn coaches and players had the LSU game circled on the schedule weeks, months in advance, they couldn't anticipate a less predictable opponent.

Before the fourth-ranked LSU Tigers could board a plane destined for Alabama and a nationally televised Saturday afternoon game, the annual arrival of hurricane season brought an unwanted visitor destined for destruction somewhere in the Gulf of Mexico. It didn't take a meteorologist to study the maps and know Hurricane Ivan was coming. It was just a matter of when and where.

When turned out to be about 2 a.m. on the Thursday before the game. Where turned out to be Gulf Shores, Alabama, before Ivan traveled North up I-65, veered Northwest into the Atlantic Ocean and circled back around before finally collapsing from exhaustion in the Gulf.

Speculation about playing the game started early in the week, followed by gamesmanship on both sides. LSU, two weeks removed from a near-miss 22-21 overtime win over Oregon State, wanted to postpone the game and play it later in the season. Auburn, 2-0 and gaining confidence from its wins over Louisiana-Monroe and Mississippi State, had no intention of letting LSU off the hook.

With classes cancelled for the week, students running for home and ESPN moving *College GameDay* from Auburn to East Lansing,

Michigan, for the Notre Dame-Michigan State game, the 14th-ranked Auburn Tigers moved to Auburn University Hotel and Conference Center in downtown Auburn.

"We had to meet something like 10 hours a day," defensive end Bret Eddins said. "We'd meet for an hour, take an hour off and then have another film session. It was all we could do because we were stuck in the hotel. We ate, played cards. A couple of guys tried to call girls and get them to come up, but they had already left town.

"There's nothing worse than just sitting around and the power was off and it was hot, but the film was still running off generators. It was a little scary, too, sitting there listening to the wind hit the windows.

"It's like going off to camp because we were stuck there all by ourselves. We ended making the best of it, so it kind of ended up being a fun thing. We made it fun, pulled a lot of practical jokes I can't really talk about."

GETTING DOWN TO BUSINESS

The Tigers also made time for practice, although their workouts had to be moved to their indoor facility, a building that includes half a field covered in artificial grass called SprinTurf. That meant only one unit could practice at a time, so the offense would never be on the field at the same time as the defense.

To the credit of the players and coaches, they worked through the temporary inconvenience. "We really aren't going to let that hold us back," cornerback Carlos Rogers said.

Auburn players also realized they weren't the only team working through difficulties that week. LSU would have to wait out the hurricane before traveling to Auburn on Friday.

"It will most definitely have an effect on both teams, because this is a game we've talked about for a while," quarterback Jason Campbell said. "You can't control the weather, so we just have to know how to adjust."

Would the preparation be enough? The coaches wanted to think so, but realistically they entered the game with genuine concerns.

"From Tuesday on we had the kids pretty much sequestered in a hotel. From Tuesday on they met, walked through [practice] inside and ate and probably played every video game imaginable, because the kids weren't allowed the leave the hotel," strength and conditioning coach Kevin Yoxall said. "From the perspective of a strength and physical coach, our preparation from a physical standpoint flew in the face of everything I've ever preached."

ONLY HALF THE WAY THERE

The first half of the LSU game looked all too familiar to frustrated Auburn fans who sat through the 2003 season wondering when and if the Tigers would ever live up to expectations.

LSU took control early when senior quarterback Marcus Randall directed an efficient opening drive, moving LSU 80 yards on 14 plays and connecting with Dwayne Bowe for a nine-yard touchdown pass with 8:23 left in the first quarter. However, kicker Ryan Gaudet missed the extra point, leaving LSU with a 6-0 lead.

Auburn then drove to the LSU five-yard line before settling for John Vaughn's 29-yard field goal with 1:37 left in the first quarter. LSU only completed one more pass the rest of the half, but that was enough to put LSU in position for a 42-yard field goal and a 9-3 halftime lead.

The halftime score suggested LSU was in control, but Auburn players knew better after spending considerable time during the week watching the film of their 2003 game at LSU, 31-7 loss that pushed LSU toward the SEC and national championships and drove Auburn toward its controversial offseason.

"We got stuck in the hotel and couldn't really practice, and we were sitting there watching film and thinking, 'Here's the defending champs just burning us, running up and down the field on us,'" Eddins said. "But by halftime we realized we were playing with them and the only thing keeping us from winning was our own mistakes.

"At that point everyone's confidence rose a little bit, and everybody's confidence in each other rose a little bit, too."

HALFTIME ADJUSTMENTS

In addition to raising their confidence to a new level at halftime of the LSU game, the Tigers also benefited from a strategic adjustment by Tuberville and defensive coordinator Gene Chizik.

Auburn came in with a complex game plan that hurt Auburn as much as it hurt LSU in the first half. At halftime Tuberville and Chizik agreed to toss out the original game plan.

"I think we blitzed too much on the first drive. I think that is the worst thing we could have done with the athletic ability of their quarterbacks, to give them a quick read," Tuberville said. "After the first drive, we decided to go to a zone and just try to play things in front of us, which makes a lot of sense because the first touchdown was a play-action pass that froze our safety and enabled their receiver to get behind him."

The halftime adjustment put the players in a position to make plays and brought out the best in a young defense searching for an identity.

"We put in all these new fancy packages to stop this and stop that," free safety Will Herring said. "And when we got in the game, they drove down the first two drives on us and had nine points like that. We went back to the basics.

"We just lined up and said, 'We're going to do what we do best, our simple stuff, and you're going to have to run the football on us.' They weren't able to do that. We stayed in our basic packages and shut everything down."

'You've Got to Believe'

The teams took turns trading the ball and field position throughout the third quarter until tailback Carnell Williams opened the door for an LSU breakthrough early in the fourth quarter. After the Auburn defense held LSU at its own 12 and forced a punt into a strong wind, Jackson's punt sailed just 13 yards. Instead of giving Auburn the ball with excellent field position, Williams let the ball bounce off his shoulder. LSU recovered at its own 45-yard line with 14:48 left in the game, and Auburn suddenly appeared to be in deep trouble.

"I remember a lot about everything late in the game," Williams said. "I had just fumbled a punt and put us in a bad position. I was down on myself and we were down 9-3 and [running backs] Coach [Eddie] Gran kept coming to me and saying, 'You've got to believe we're going to win 10-9.' He was so intense, 'You've got to believe—10-9, 10-9!'"

*Courtney Taylor's touchdown reception against LSU proved to be
one of the the key turning points of Auburn's season.*
Scott Cunningham/Getty Images

"I told him to get ready," Gran said. "I told him we were going to win the game 10-9, and he was going to make a big play to help make it happen."

Gran's message turned out to be prophetic—for both Williams and his teammates.

ONE LAST CHANCE

The Auburn defense continued to hold up its end, forcing two more punts and giving the offense yet another opportunity at its own 40-yard line with 6:37 left in the game. If the offense was ever going to move forward after a year of frustration and do its part to make Auburn a championship contender, the time had arrived to get the job done.

"We knew we could make our season right here," Campbell said.

No one understood that better than Campbell, who endured considerable criticism and blame throughout the 2003 season and still had so much to prove—not only to the fans, but to his coaches, teammates and himself.

"Jason stepped into the huddle and said, 'Y'all get me the best protection you can give, because we're fixin' to go down and score and win the game,'" guard Danny Lindsey said. "We believed him. We believed in each other."

"Before that last drive, Jason came into the huddle and looked at us and said, 'This is it. This is all we've got. We've got one shot. Let's get it done,'" Williams said. "And he delivered."

Campbell's clutch delivery didn't come without its struggles. After an incomplete pass, a 20-yard run by Ronnie Brown and a six-yard run by Brown, Williams finally made good on Gran's prediction. Facing second-and-four at the LSU 33, Campbell threw a screen pass toward Williams, but LSU cornerback Corey Webster jumped the play and had the ball in his hands for a brief moment before Williams grabbed it away. The play gained only three yards, but, it turns out, it saved the drive and most likely the game and the season.

"That's the kind of player he is," Tuberville said of Williams. "He's football smart. He understood the play and how it was unfolding and what he had to do. There were several plays on that drive that could have gone the other way if guys didn't make the right decisions."

One of those guys was Campbell, who scrambled four yards on the next play for a first down at LSU's 26. After Williams suffered a two-yard loss on the next play and Campbell's next two passes failed to reach Ben Obomanu, Auburn faced fourth and 12 with 3:07 left in the game.

"We called a timeout and we were just trying to get the best possible play to get Jason away from the rush because LSU was coming with the blitz the whole game," receiver Courtney Taylor said.

Campbell dropped back, rolled to his right, met immediate resistance from the LSU blitz and side-armed a pass toward Taylor.

"We had a play called 'Knock Nine comeback' with two comebacks on the outside, with me and Anthony Mix," Taylor said. "It's about a 16-yard route and we needed 12, so I took off, the corner—I think it was [LSU cornerback] Travis Daniels—was with me kind of tight and I made my break and the ball was on the way. Travis was there, but Jason made a great throw, and I was able to make a play on it."

Still, even Taylor wasn't sure if it was enough.

"I thought I had a first down," Taylor said. "But I had to run out of the break because he [Daniels] was right there on me, so I looked up just to see."

Campbell never got the chance to see the play, but the result was obvious.

"I heard the crowd and I knew it was good," Taylor said. "First down. Move the chains."

Looking back, that might have been the play of the year for the Tigers.

"That was the play," offensive coordinator Al Borges said. "Jason was under duress and threw the ball outside to Courtney Taylor. That was the drive."

The drive was not complete. Not even close. Three plays later, facing third and 12 at the LSU 16, the Tigers found themselves in another dangerous situation.

"Jason definitely showed a lot of leadership right there," tight end Cooper Wallace said. "He kept talking to us in the huddle, calming us down, telling us we need to play a make and get it done."

Lined up one-on-one with LSU nickelback Ronnie Prude Taylor ran five yards and faked a route to the sideline.

"He bit," Taylor said.

With Prude going out for the out pattern, Taylor turned his route upfield and into the end zone and waited for Campbell's perfect pass to arrive.

"It was coming so slowly and I was just saying, 'Come on, get here, ball,'" Taylor said. "At the same time I was just praying, 'Please God, let me catch this ball. I'm too wide open. I don't want to drop it.' There was a lot of everything going through my mind."

There was also the ball, in his hands, in his arms, secured to his chest, in the end zone for a touchdown and a 9-9 tie with 1:14 left in the game.

"It was a huge sigh of relief," Campbell said. "We knew if we kept plugging, something would happen."

THE COLOR YELLOW

All Auburn had to do to take the lead was kick the extra point, a relatively simple task considering Auburn entered the game having converted 191 consecutive extra-point attempts, dating back to 1999 for the second longest streak in SEC history.

Instead, Auburn turned a routine PAT into a near-disaster when snapper Pete Compton rolled the ball back to holder Sam Rives and kicker John Vaughn's kick sailed mercilessly, painfully left.

"It was brutal," Rives said. "My heart sank."

Just two weeks earlier, Auburn players watched on television as Oregon State kicker Alexis Serna missed three extra points in a one-point overtime loss to LSU.

"I didn't have Jon Vaughn's number so I called [backup kicker] Phillip Yost and told him, 'Tell Vaughn if he ever misses an extra point like that and we lose I'm gonna kick his butt,'" Eddins said. "I was just kidding around, but then in the LSU game I'm out there on the extra-point team and I hear the kick and turn around and see that it's no good and I just turned around and looked at him and I'm just thinking 'Oh my . . . how is this happening?'

"I had this awful feeling in the pit of my stomach. Then I saw the flag."

A year earlier, the flag would have stayed in the official's pocket. In 2004, due to a new and relatively obscure rule, the flag flew when Prude jumped over the line of scrimmage and landed on Compton.

"[There] couldn't possibly be a bigger relief than that little yellow thing on the ground," Vaughn said.

With a second chance, Auburn's kicking unit had a chance to collect its breath and get it right. That wasn't enough to save Compton, who rolled another snap, but it was all Rives needed to gather the ball, get it set and in position when Vaughn's leg sailed through and sent the ball between the uprights for the winning points.

"Sometimes in a good season," Tuberville said, "you just have to have lucky things go your way."

Then again, as the old coaches' axiom insists, luck is when preparation meets opportunity. When Auburn got a second chance, it was prepared to make the most of its opportunity.

THE ULTIMATE TURNING POINT?

When Auburn coaches and players look back on the 2004 season, they see a number of important turning points that all played a part in a perfect season. None could be more significant than the game-winning drive against LSU and what it ultimately meant for Campbell, the offense, the defense, the special teams—the entire team.

"That was a defining moment for our team when Jason stepped up and showed everybody he could make plays, that he was the leader of our offense and was willing to take on the pressure that comes along with being quarterback," Brown said. "Everybody knew it was going to be a hard-fought game and we were going to have to make plays to win that game and there's nothing bigger than making a big play on fourth and 12 late in the game.

"I think the way we won that game was a defining moment that carried over to the rest of the season. It showed what we were capable of as a team and sort of unified us."

For Campbell, the LSU game announced his arrival as a game-winning senior quarterback.

"The guys on the team know that I've taken a lot of unfair criticism over the years," Campbell said. "Those two plays in the fourth quarter say a lot about my character and the team's character."

For the offense, the game-winning drive proved to be the confidence boost that had been missing for so long.

"It was early in the season, and we weren't a well-oiled machine offensively. We had a way to go," Borges said. "The way we won the game is what turned us a little bit—knowing our quarterback brought us back and our defense played fabulously to keep us in it."

For the defense, the entire second half provided the confirmation of what the coaches and players had suspected all along.

"It clicked, to me, after the LSU game when we just never gave up," defensive end Doug Langenfeld said. "LSU scored on their first drive of the game and then they got a field goal to make it nine, but after that we just got our heads back together, calmed everybody down, started getting LSU off the field and came through in the end. After that, we knew we had what it took to be special."

For the entire team, it became the point in time in which the Tigers began to see themselves as a true championship contender, even if they didn't say it out loud at the time.

"When we beat LSU I knew we were capable of winning a national championship," strong safety Junior Rosegreen said. "That's when I knew we could be a special team.

"We knew we still had to win at Tennessee and beat Georgia at home to have a special year. We knew we still had a long way to go, but at least we felt like we really had a chance."

At the time, though, the Tigers couldn't afford to get caught up in turning points, rankings and championship talk. They were only 3-0 with eight games left in the regular season.

"Is this a turning point? No, I think it's just a point that people will recognize that we've got a pretty decent team and things are going to just heat up on us," Tuberville said the day after the LSU game. "We're going to see if we can handle it."

CHAPTER 7

Jason Campbell: Proving His Point

On the surface, in front of the cameras, surrounded by the note-books and tape recorders, besieged by the children seeking autographs and the fans hoping to shake his hand and pat his back, Jason Campbell tried to pretend the past didn't hurt.

"It bothered me sometimes what people said about me, but I tried not to take it personally," Campbell said. "The quarterback always gets the finger pointed at him. You can't let that mess with your whole career."

At least that's what he said in public, when he had to put on his best face, look straight ahead and act as if nothing had happened. In private, behind the surface, Campbell sat down for an interview in late December of his senior year, set his eyes on dead serious, reached into his heart and pulled out a statement that reflected the pain of a college career scarred by doubts, questions and criticism.

"I always knew I could be the kind of quarterback who could take a team to a championship," Campbell said. "I did it in high school, and I knew I could do it in college.

"Before people always criticized me for not winning the big game, but go back and look at some of the big games where I helped put us in the right position to win the big game. Look at the Alabama games the two years before [2002 and 2003]. Other times I put us in the right positions to win games and we didn't finish. That wasn't my fault. I did my job, but when you don't win the game people point to the quarterback.

"Even though I wasn't feeling a lot of heat from my coaches and teammates from 'not winning the big games' it still hurt when other people didn't recognize I was doing my job and it wasn't my fault we weren't winning all those games. People acted like I was the one person losing those games. That's what hurt.

"So when we won the LSU game, it felt like a mountain had been lifted off my shoulders. I felt like I had proved something I always knew was true."

There was a time when Campbell's critics gave up on him, but Campbell refused to give up. There was a time when Campbell's critics hoped he would give way to another quarterback, but Campbell refused to go away.

Then, when it mattered most, there was a time when Campbell finally put it all together and proved what he had known all along, driving Auburn 59 yards on 12 plays, completing a 14-yard pass on fourth and 12 and a 16-yard touchdown on third and 12 in the final minutes of a decisive 10-9 victory over LSU.

"All the criticism he took, most folks would have run out of town," tailback Carnell Williams said. "For Jason to turn around and lead us to a game-winning touchdown. . . ."

Williams didn't finish the sentence. He didn't have to. Campbell's teammates knew. They had known all along.

"He's been this good for a while now—at least in my eyes," center Jeremy Ingle said late in the 2004 season. "The leadership and the accuracy have been there since I've known him. I think now he's just more comfortable with what's going on. He looks better to a lot of people, I guess, but it's just the same old Jason to us."

A LONG AND WINDING ROAD

Campbell traveled a complex path through five up-and-down years at Auburn, starting when he arrived 2000 as a Parade All-American from Taylorsville, Mississippi. At six foot five, 220 pounds with the ability to pass and run, he was seen as the answer. After redshirting his first fall at Auburn, it wasn't long before Campbell was surrounded by questions.

He played in all 10 games that season, started eight games and passed for 1,117 yards with four touchdowns and four interceptions while sharing the job with Daniel Cobb, but Auburn's general lack of offensive consistency and his own inexperience didn't do anything to build Campbell's confidence. In fact, Campbell seriously considered transferring.

"My redshirt year I tried to please everybody because I was so highly recruited as a Parade All-American in high school," Campbell said. "Everyone expects so much out of you and you try to play up to those expectations. That was my first mistake."

After coach Tommy Tuberville fired offensive coordinator Noel Mazzone following the 2001 season and replaced him with Bobby Petrino, Campbell once again spent the 2002 season sharing the job with Cobb, playing in all 13 games, starting six and passing for 11 touchdowns with five interceptions.

When Cobb graduated and Petrino became the head coach at Louisville following the 2002 season, Campbell prepared himself for a shot to become the full-time starting quarterback and another coaching change. This time Tuberville attempted to keep Petrino's offense intact by promoting offensive line Hugh Nall to coordinator and hiring Steve Ensminger to coach quarterbacks and help coach the plays.

"When you go to college, you're hoping you have the opportunity to have one coordinator for the four years," Campbell said. "Because if you do that, you have the opportunity to graduate from point A to point B each year, and you keep improving. My situation has been kind of different. I've changed coordinators each year."

The Tigers entered the 2003 season with a No. 1 ranking in two preseason polls and Campbell as the starting quarterback, but the high expectations surrounding the season soon fell apart under the weight of a 23-0 loss to USC in the opener and a 17-3 loss to Georgia Tech in the second game. Campbell went on to pass for 2,267 yards with 10 touchdowns and eight interceptions, but the Tigers finished 8-5, and Campbell became an easy target for criticism along with Tuberville, Nall and Ensminger.

"It's just a matter of when you're losing, you're always going to get the blame if you're the quarterback," Campbell said.

A World of Potential

When Tuberville demoted Nall and Ensminger and replaced them with veteran offensive coordinator Al Borges in January 2004, it didn't take Borges long to see Campbell had the makings of a special quarterback.

"I saw a world of potential with the kid," Borges said. "He could get the ball there and he'd been well coached. In fact, he'd been exposed to so many good coaches that it increased his learning curve. But not being able to work in the same system, that hurts you."

Campbell's initial steps under Borges were not without their stumbles. In fact, there were times in the spring when Campbell accidentally found himself using calls and terminology from former Auburn offensive systems.

"Coach Borges let me know every time I did it, and the guys in the huddle would start laughing," Campbell said. "I could be a good coach. I could put in the 995 different plays that I ran in college. It would probably be a good offense."

It wasn't long before Campbell began to pick up Borges's offensive system and make it his own.

"It didn't take long at all, maybe two or three weeks into spring ball," Campbell said. "We started learning a bunch of things that we haven't done here. For a quarterback, you get an opportunity to make plays and the people around you get the opportunity to make plays.

"It seems all of the pressure wasn't just on the quarterback to make all of the plays. You could relax and have fun."

Stepping Up, Stepping Out

Campbell still had some important steps to take. He not only had to prove he could do his part in the passing game to make Auburn a productive offense, but he also had to prove he could be the leader the Tigers needed him to be.

Strong safety Junior Rosegreen told Campbell before the season, "We need you to lead. You've got to be like Michael Jordan and say, 'Coach, I want the ball in my hands.'"

Slowly but surely Campbell came out of his shell and emerged as a more vocal force for the Tigers, rallying his teammates in the huddle, calling player-only meetings and, most important, taking over in the critical moments of games. Campbell was at his best in the LSU game when he stepped into the huddle with Auburn trailing 9-3 and 6:37 left in the game and told his teammates the time had come to take control and win the game.

"When I heard Jason say that," wide receiver Courtney Taylor said, "I knew it was our time."

Campbell helped make it Auburn's time by completing two critical passes, connecting with Taylor on fourth and 16 for a first down and third and 12 for a touchdown with LSU defenders bearing down.

"Just him standing in there and three or four guys in his face and on his back while he's getting rid of the ball and completing the pass," Williams said. "That's something I'll always cherish."

It also became something Auburn coaches and teammates came to expect through the course of Campbell's senior season.

"You knew he was going to be able to handle tough situations, and he did that for us," Tuberville said. "I couldn't be any prouder for him."

GROWING BY THE GAME

In Borges's offense, Campbell's improvement became more and more apparent with each game. Time and time again, defenses decided to concentrate their efforts on stopping Auburn's running game. Time and time again, Campbell made them pay, checking off to the right play and making the play with his experience and his arm instead of taking off and running as he had so often earlier in his career.

"He committed himself to being a passer," Borges said. "When I came here we sat down and said, 'We're going to do all we can to make you a good passer. That's really where you're going to help this team win. You run for yards, but you throw for miles.'"

Campbell did that just, especially in the season's biggest games. In the victory at Tennessee, he completed 15 of 21 passes for 240 yards in the first half alone, leading Auburn to a 31-3 halftime lead. Against Arkansas he completed 17 of 19 passes for 297 yards and three touchdowns. Against Georgia he completed 18 of 22 passes for 189 yards and a touchdown. He also took a vicious hit to the head just as he tossed an option pitch to Williams, who ran untouched for Auburn's first touchdown of the game.

In the Alabama game, he rallied Auburn to victory in the second half and completed 18 of 24 passes for 224 yards and a touchdown. Against Tennessee in the SEC championship game he turned his game up another few notches, completing 27 of 35 passes for 374 yards and three touchdowns. He topped it all off with another strong performance in the Sugar Bowl, he came through with several big plays and completed 11 of 16 passes for 189 yards and a touchdown against Virginia Tech.

"Jason's done it every time we needed him to," Borges said. "He's a confident athletic player, and there's nothing more dangerous than a confident athletic player."

STIFF-ARMED BY THE HEISMAN

Near the end of the season, Borges insisted Campbell's name belonged near the top of the list of Heisman Trophy contenders.

"Tell me who is playing better," Borges says. "If you can tell me who is playing better, from what they're asked to do . . . remember he ain't throwing 40 passes a game. That would be bad coaching if we did. Who is playing better? Who has led their team? Who has had the largest margin of victory? That's all him.

"And it's not just passing. The passing is the thing that everybody notices. The thing about Jason is he gets you in and out of good and bad plays on a consistent basis. It doesn't matter if there are 83,000 [opposing fans] screaming in the stands or there's 87,000 in our stadium. He's always the same."

Unfortunately for Campbell, an invitation to attend the Heisman Trophy ceremony in New York never arrived.

13 STEPS TO A LEGACY

Somebody noticed. Campbell still received the SEC Offensive Player of the Year award from both the SEC and The Associated Press, as well as first-team All-SEC honors from both groups after finishing third in the nation in passing efficiency, with 2,700 yards, 188 completions on 270 attempts (69.63 percent), 20 touchdowns and seven interceptions. He also developed into a consistent big-play threat, completing 40 passes for 20 or more yards.

His most important numbers, however, came in the form of 13 wins, zero losses and one SEC championship. In his media guide bio, he wrote his biggest dream was "winning a championship." In 2004, he made his dream come true.

"Stats don't mean a whole lot if you're not winning," Campbell said. "You may throw for 400 yards, but if you lose a game, it's a losing cause.

"As a team you sweat together and work all summer to win games. You are trying to do everything you can to win a game. That's all I wanted to do."

Along the way he also left a legacy for future Tigers to follow, especially Auburn's quarterbacks.

"I think this season said a lot about my character," Campbell said. "It says my teammates believed in me, my coaches believed in me. . . . Maybe people will lay off me. I've always played hard. But people don't see it unless you win. Fortunately, people see it now."

CHAPTER 8

The Citadel: Get It Done

With Auburn moving from 14th to ninth in the national polls after its victory over LSU, the Tigers faced a dangerous opponent the next week—and it wasn't The Citadel.

"Part of my job as a head coach is to get our guys to understand that you to forget about last week's game," head coach Tommy Tuberville said. "I told them Sunday afternoon [after the LSU game] they'll get a lot of handshakes and pats on the back. That always happens when you win a game like this. But it doesn't mean a whole lot if you don't respond the next week and forget about it and go on."

As soon as Auburn defeated LSU, outsiders had to start wondering if the Tigers would fall into a familiar historical pattern of struggling with high expectations. Auburn has typically played its best football as an underdog, but now the Tigers had emerged as the surprising favorite to win the SEC West.

Drawing on their 2003 experience as preseason favorites proved to be a positive for the Tigers.

"A lot of the guys have been reminding each other of last year," defensive end Bret Eddins said. "We're the guys with the targets on our backs now and we've been there before. It didn't always go very well. I hope what happened last year will make us work harder."

Cornerback Carlos Rogers added, "We're staying calm, staying focused and not looking ahead. We thought we were the best last year. We hadn't been in that situation before. Now we know you can't be overexcited or overconfident about things like rankings."

As the Tigers showed in 2003, that's easier said than done. Could these Tigers handle their new role?

"The LSU game just shows everybody how good we are," tailback Carnell Williams said. "Last year we were predicted to do some great things. I've been telling everybody that I feel like this is our year to do great things. Some of the things we didn't do last year we're going to accomplish this year.

"We're not a fluke. We came to play ball. We're coming for the SEC West, the SEC championship, whatever."

Whatever? The Tigers had to get past The Citadel first.

TAKING CARE OF BUSINESS

Here's how it's supposed to work: Division I-AA team plays at major college power. Division I-AA team gets paycheck. Major college power gets easy win. Every once in a while, though, both teams forget to play their roles and upsets happen.

Auburn fans had to wonder when the two teams traded turnovers on their first possessions, and when the Bulldogs drove to the Auburn 25-yard line on their second possession before missing a field goal. Then the teams reverted to their traditional roles with Auburn driving for a touchdown, blocking a punt for a safety before the end of the first quarter and adding two more touchdowns by halftime. By the time it was all over, the Tigers had cleared the bench and won 33-3.

So much for stumbling under the weight of a top-10 ranking. The Tigers practiced hard throughout the week and didn't just go through the motions against the Bulldogs, an approach that would become a pattern throughout the season.

"We took care of business," Tuberville said. "It wasn't anything exciting. It was just one of those days when we went out and got it done. I could tell the focus was on a little bit different team than the one we were playing today."

A different team? Such as . . . Tennessee, Auburn's next opponent?

A DIFFERENT KIND OF TURNING POINT

When the Tigers reflect back on the 2004 season, it's easy to point to the summer conditioning, the LSU game, the Tennessee game and other dramatic moments as turning points. But beating The Citadel? Actually, it was Carnell Williams who looked back and insisted the game against The Citadel was something of a turning point and he made a good point.

"We came out and took the game seriously and took care of our business," Williams said. "It was a game kind of stuck between two big games, and we needed to play well so we didn't lose any momentum, so I thought it was kind of a big game for us."

Best of all, it helped the Tigers get ready for another big game against a top-10 team.

"We definitely know we still haven't arrived," Williams said. "We felt like we were there last year at the start of the season, but we didn't come out and play. Look what happened.

"The minute you think you've arrived, someone knocks you on your back."

CHAPTER 9

The Running Backs: Unselfishly Sharing the Spotlight

They're too good to be true. They can't be for real. No one really acts, thinks or feels that way, even if they say it over and over. Today's star players aren't supposed to be that unselfish. They're not supposed to be that team-oriented. They're not supposed to be that humble and genuine.

At least that's what NFL scouts and coaches thought when they met Carnell Williams and Ronnie Brown as they prepared for the 2005 NFL Draft. Scouts and coaches are supposed to be skeptical and look for every potential flaw in a player's physical, mental and emotional makeup. The harder they looked, the more they came to see something genuinely special in Auburn's terrific tailback tandem.

"We all see their talents, but as you talk to them, that's when they move up even more," Chicago Bears head coach Lovie Smith said. "We know a few coaches down there [at Auburn]. What we'd heard initially, you wanted to see it for yourself, and that's what it was—you talk about unselfish.

"I mean, most of the time, running backs say, 'Hey, I'm the man, give me the ball.' You've got Ronnie Brown lining up as a fullback. How many great tailbacks line up as a fullback? He's also on the punt team. You talk to both of them. They want to give the other guy a lot of credit. They're both special players."

That's nothing new to the coaches and players at Auburn. They already knew that. If anyone didn't know it for sure, they certainly saw it in during the 2004 season when Williams and Brown defied today's "me first" culture during one of the most inspiring seasons in modern college football.

"These guys have been great not only for our team, but for the SEC and college football," Auburn head coach Tommy Tuberville said. "How they've played, how they've handled themselves, their unselfish acts on and off the football field are going to have a drastic trickle-down effect for our younger players over the next few years."

One More Time

It's hard to imagine Auburn going 13-0 and winning the SEC championship in 2004 without Williams and Brown doing their part, both on and off the field, but Tuberville and the coaching staff had to consider the possibility when they hit the recruiting trail in December 2003.

The coaches knew both running backs had asked the NFL to evaluate their status for the 2004 draft. They also knew that while it was likely one would leave for the NFL and the other would stay, it was also possible both would pass up their senior season to enter the NFL draft. Then again, there was also the extraordinary but still hopeful possibility they might both defy the odds and decide to return.

"When you've got two NFL-caliber backs, most guys would get together and say, 'If you do this, I'm going to do that, and if you do that I'm going to do that,'" Williams said. "The whole time we were making our decision we were trying to communicate with each other, how we felt, what we were thinking.

"Then we sort of went our separate ways, talked to our families and then we came back together and talked and we both had the same idea."

People outside the program tried to warn Williams and Brown about the prospect of co-existing as seniors. They told them there wouldn't be enough carries to go around to satisfy both backs. Instead of listening to every voice with a whispered concern, the two listened to their families, their coaches, NFL executives—and each other.

"We talked about it a little bit, knowing we were in the same situation and playing the same position and having some of the same goals," Brown said. "So we talked about it a little bit and tried to give each other a little insight, but ultimately it was going to be a personal decision—his decision and my decision."

Neither knew the other's decision until minutes before it came time to make an announcement on January 14, 2004. Both recall dropping hints in their conversations, but neither one has a clear recollection of who told whom first.

"I had talked to him a couple of days before and we both felt pretty comfortable about coming back," Brown said. "We had both talked to NFL scouts and they had some questions about us as football players, and it was in our best interests to come back.

"The one thing my parents said is if you make a decision, stick with it and try not to second-guess yourself. Once I decided to come back, I was really pretty comfortable with my decision."

Both players admit the chance to win a championship was a primary reason for their return.

"My first two years I was hurt, and I never got the full college atmosphere," Williams said. "For me to play one good year last year and to know how much fun it was when we were 8-5, I thought, 'Imagine what it would be like to play for an SEC championship, what a great feeling that would be.'"

Once they had made their decisions, the first step was to tell Tuberville.

"I was kind of leaning toward staying in school the whole time anyway, but in the end it just kind of came together," Williams said. "We walked up to Coach Tuberville's office before the press conference. He wanted to know what we had decided before we announced it. You could see by looking at his face he was kind of nervous."

"When we walked into Coach Tuberville's office he was pretty nervous because he didn't know what we were going to do," Brown said. "When we told him, he gave us a sigh of relief and he said, 'OK, let's get started on the season.'"

The next step came with a press conference.

"It was a quiet thing up until right before the press conference, with both of us going back and forth, leaning one way at times and thinking

*The unselfish attitudes of Carnell Williams, left,
and Ronnie Bown set an example for the Tigers.*
Photo by Todd J. Van Emst

about something else at other times," Brown said. "It varied for both of us. I know for a while I was leaning toward going if he decided to come back. Ultimately, I think we both felt like if we were meant to play in the NFL, it would happen when it happens."

As Tuberville has said on numerous occasions since January 14, "That was a great day for Auburn."

NO PASSING FANCY

The next step for Williams and Brown was meeting with new offensive coordinator Al Borges to alleviate their concerns about his West Coast offense. When Tuberville brought Borges in nearly a month after Williams and Brown decided to stay, both players immediately found themselves wondering what it meant for the running game. When they thought of the West Coast offense, they thought of Joe Montana and Steve Young passing the ball for coach Bill Walsh and the San Francisco 49ers. They did not, however, see the potential for two backs to each touch the ball 15-20 times per game.

Turns out they were wrong, and Borges wasted little time letting them know he had no intentions of throwing the ball 50 times a game and abandoning the running game.

"I told them there was no way we were going to turn this thing into a passing circus," Borges said. "I told them this wasn't a finesse offense, that we still had to be physical and run the ball. I also told them the same thing I had told Tommy when I interviewed for the job, that I really thought we could find a way to make the best use of both players as runners, receivers and blockers."

It was one thing to say it. It was another to actually do it, and Williams and Brown soon found themselves playing a variety of roles, even playing together at times when Brown entered the game as a fullback or slot receiver.

"During spring football, we spent an inordinate amount of time figuring out how we could play both at the same time because they are both so highly skilled," Borges said. "Ronnie has great receiving skills as well as running skills, and as for Carnell, I don't think I need to tell you what his capabilities are.

"I was brought up watching Roger Craig play with the 49ers. When Ronnie, who is 234 pounds, walked in the room, I started seeing Roger Craig. He was a big leg lifter just like Roger was a big leg lifter. Ronnie's style of running is different, but the way he plays the position is so similar to Roger. He has great hands, great burst of speed, good blocker, [Roger] played fullback half his career when Wendell Tyler was there, played halfback when Tom Rathman was there; I just saw a lot of him in Ronnie. So we tried to build our offense in that image a little bit, in Roger Craig's image from my own perspective."

For that to happen, Borges would need two unselfish backs willing to share the ball, the position and the spotlight.

SHARE AND SHARE ALIKE

Competitive conflict seemed almost inevitable for Williams and Brown. It was Brown who arrived at Auburn first in 2000 after a career as one of Georgia's top prep running backs. After redshirting during the 2000 season, Brown met Williams when Williams visited campus during a recruiting trip.

"Someone told me that's who he was," Williams said. "They said, 'This is Ronnie Brown. He's one of our running backs.' We shook hands and went our way."

Neither one really thought much of it until Williams arrived on campus after a Parade All-American career at Etowah High School in Attalla, Alabama. Williams soon realized who Brown was and quickly decided, "I'm in kind of a bad situation here. We're both freshmen. I said, 'This guy is pretty good. Man, I'm going to have to get out here and work, 'cause man, this guy's got skills. He can play this game. I didn't feel like I was screwed, but I said, 'It's going to be a great competition.'"

Brown not only welcomed the competition but welcomed Williams himself.

"When I got here as a freshman, I came in with a big-time name, supposed to do this and that," Williams said. "Ronnie didn't show any animosity toward me. He helped me out, like out on the field, trying to understand plays. He was always there for me, and that shows what kind of guy he was."

Brown's positive attitude never wavered, even when Williams quickly passed him on the depth chart. Brown ended spring 2001 as the team's starting tailback, and they both earned SEC All-Freshman honors that fall, but it was Williams who started six games and led the team in rushing with 614 yards, while Brown rushed for 330.

Williams continued to build on his success through the first half of the 2002 season until he suffered a broken ankle in the seventh game at Florida. In that same game, Brown stepped in and finished with 163 yards and two touchdowns. By the time the season was over he had rushed for 1,008 yards and 13 touchdowns in his half of the season, while Williams finished with 745 yards and 10 touchdowns in his half.

Between nagging injuries, Auburn's offensive struggles and Williams rushing for 1,307 yards and 17 touchdowns, Brown finished with 446 yards and five touchdowns in 2003 but still maintained his positive approach toward Williams and his own role on the team.

"It's been kind of weird," Brown said. "Most of the time you come in and play, and then things just kind of go up. But I had to face a little adversity from time to time."

Through it all, "He's never been in my office [complaining] one time," running backs coach Eddie Gran said. "If anybody had a gripe, it would have been him. He could have come to my office and said, 'Coach, why am I not getting carries? What's the deal here?' Never. Not one time. In our society, that doesn't happen very often."

PARTNERSHIP PAYS OFF

The team-first partnership of Brown and Williams played a critical role in making the Tigers so successful in 2004.

In addition to Brown's impressive combination of size, strength and speed at six foot one, 233 pounds, and Williams's remarkable mix of quickness, vision and toughness that belies his size at 5-10, 205 pounds, both players proved themselves as receivers and blockers while playing special teams and sharing the backfield and the spotlight without flinching.

"It's very rare—you just don't see players of that caliber who aren't constantly complaining about getting the ball more," Borges says. "They've been a microcosm of the entire football team. We have a lot of unselfishness on this team and we wouldn't be 12-0 if we didn't have it. If we had featured one back and given him 30 carries a game, we'd probably have a Heisman Trophy winner."

Williams did his part by carrying 239 times for 1,236 yards, 4.9 yards per carry and 12 touchdowns, while Brown missed one game [against The Citadel] with an injury and carried 153 times for 928 yards, 6.0 yards per carry and eight touchdowns. Brown also emerged as Auburn's second-leading receiver with 34 receptions for 313 yards and a touchdown, while Williams caught 21 passes for 152 yards and a touchdown.

Because Williams came to Auburn with the nickname "Cadillac" the media decided Brown needed his own nickname. Some called him "Hummer." Others called him "Escalade." Either way, he emerged from Williams's shadow as a senior.

"We've always known how good Ronnie is," center Jeremy Ingle said. "He's one of the best backs in the country—top three, in my opinion. He's the total package, he really is."

Between their individual achievements and the team's success, both Brown and Williams completed their Auburn careers confident they had done the right thing by returning for their senior seasons.

"I knew it could happen because of the type of people me and Ronnie are," Williams said. "We're more about team, more about winning. But I never thought it would work out like it did, with both of us doing real well. It's sweet."

Brown added, "Looking back on it, I'm glad I did it. Some of the things we've done this season, I'm glad I didn't miss any of it. I'm looking forward to the future, too."

Chapter 10

Tennessee: A Volatile Mix

The victory over LSU proved Auburn could beat a top team at home, but the Tigers still had something to prove about their ability to win a momentous road game. They would get that chance on October 2, in front of more than 107,000 in Tennessee's Neyland Stadium.

Before the eighth-ranked Tigers reached Knoxville to be greeted by the 10th-ranked Vols, the ESPN GameDay crew and a national television audience, they prepared themselves for the largest and loudest stadium they would face all season.

"Loud is loud," receiver Anthony Mix said. "Anywhere you go it's loud."

Instead of focusing on Tennessee's noise and endless renditions of "Rocky Top," the Tigers focused on their own plans. Having already experienced an attempt to blast crowd noise at practice when he was a University of Miami assistant in the 1980s, Auburn head coach Tommy Tuberville wasn't about to let his team get fixated on factors they couldn't control.

"I still have a headache from that," Tuberville said. "I don't think it serves any purpose. What you do is talk about focus and communication with your team all week long. We've been to several stadiums before that are very noisy. It just takes a lot more concentration."

It also helps to have a mature team growing more confident with each practice, each game.

"We have a lot of experience right now," senior center Jeremy Ingle said. "We can go into hostile environments, and you know the guy next to you can handle a hostile environment. Nobody's going to freak out on you."

Forget the rankings, the crowd, the noise and the television audience. The Tigers had only one thing on their minds as they prepared for Tennessee.

"Every week we're just trying to fight our hardest," offensive tackle Marcus McNeill said. "We're just hungry and thirsty and ready to eat. When you've got a group of guys like that that's willing to fight with you every down, then only you can hold yourself back."

FRIDAY NIGHT LIGHT

When the Tigers arrived in Knoxville they had no idea the team would undergo a dramatic and defining moment nearly 24 hours before they played the Vols.

At the team's usual Friday night devotional, chaplain Chette Williams spoke to the team about Roman soldiers who entered battle connected by hooks on their waists. He took the lesson one step further by challenging the players to take the same attitude when they took the field together against Tennessee. Then reserve tight end Kyle Derozan shared a song he had sung at his church. The song, "Hard Fighting Soldiers," opened eyes, ears and hearts.

"The night before the game in our prayer meeting at the hotel we hooked up and really bonded," wide receiver Devin Aromashodu said. "That was the first time we sang 'Hard Fighting Soldiers.' We hooked up like the Roman soldiers did and sang the song and told each other we were there for each other and we really believed in each other. We made sure when we went out there we really had each other's back. That was probably the game right there."

BRING ON THE VOLS

Despite his performance against LSU and his growing confidence and effectiveness, Auburn's Jason Campbell wasn't the quarterback in the spotlight in the days and hours leading up to the game. Instead, national and regional media outlets, especially ESPN's *GameDay*, focused their attention on Tennessee's talented true freshmen quarterbacks Erik Ainge and Brent Schaeffer.

"All day long I heard about those two other quarterbacks on television and they never mentioned Jason," Tuberville said.

Tuberville and his coaches knew the announcers were making a mistake. For one thing, the offensive coaches showed their faith in Campbell by convincing Tuberville the day before the game to allow Campbell to be audible at the line of scrimmage. Despite concerns about the noise at Neyland Stadium, offensive coordinator Al Borges instructed Campbell to treat the game like any other game when it came to changing plays at the last second.

It also helped that the Auburn coaches were convinced Tennessee's commitment to stopping the run would expose the emerging flaws in the Vols' young, inexperienced secondary.

"We really hadn't attempted to attack any secondary up until that point," Tuberville said.

On the other side of the ball, Auburn's defensive coaches were convinced they could show enough looks and apply enough pressure to create chaos for both Ainge and Schaeffer. As if the defense needed any extra motivation, Ainge did his part early in the week when he wondered out loud about the toughness of Auburn's secondary.

"We wanted to get after Ainge, because he was talking a lot of trash in the paper and that hurt us," strong safety Junior Rosegreen said. "We knew he was signing a big check that he couldn't cash. We had to make sure he couldn't cash that check."

THREE FOR THREE

The coaches turned out to be right on all three fronts, and Auburn's volatile mix of team strengths set the tone early. Campbell did his part in the first half by completing 12 of 15 passes for an extraordinary 240 yards and two touchdowns. Auburn went on to take 11 plays at least 10 yards and six plays at least 25 yards in the first half alone as Campbell checked to deep pass plays early enough to get the new play to all of his offensive teammates and make the Vols pay for crowding the line.

"People don't realize how well he actually did," Tuberville said of Campbell. "Most of the plays he threw down the field he checked to."

More important, Campbell continued to show critics what his coaches and teammates already believed.

"I had heard about how good their quarterbacks were, but I wouldn't trade either one of them for ours," Tuberville said. "He controlled the crowd. He executed. He did an outstanding job with mental preparation. He was tough. Jason doesn't make mistakes."

Those "other" quarterbacks couldn't say the same thing that night. When Ainge and Schaeffer attempted to pass, they found more resistance than they had experienced in their young careers. Auburn only recorded one sack but caused enough disruptions to force Ainge into four interceptions and Schaeffer into one of his own.

"We knew they were young and they hadn't faced a defense like us," Rosegreen said. "We had to come out and put some pressure on them and that's what we did. [Ainge] was showing us where he was throwing the ball."

JUNIOR ACHIEVEMENT

When Ainge started giving himself away, no one was in a better position to make him pay than Rosegreen. Perhaps Rosegreen should have seen it coming, because his father, Normao, had predicted he would have a big game the night before the Tigers played the Vols.

"He just felt in his heart that I would get two or more interceptions," Rosegreen said. "When he told me that, I was shocked, but it was more shocking when I actually did it. When I got my first interception, I thought about what he said, and that's when I went into my zone to make big things happen."

Between his first interception of the game, two minutes into the second quarter, and his dad's prediction, it didn't take long for Rosegreen's confidence to jump.

"I was telling everybody I was going to get three," Rosegreen said. "When I got two, they were like, 'Man, you can get another one.' When I got that third one, they were like, 'I think you're going to get another one.'"

Turns out they were right. Rosegreen finished with four interceptions, tying an SEC record and breaking Auburn's mark. Add a fumble recovery and he went on to become the SEC's Defensive Player of the Week.

"I don't think we had four all year in 2003," Tuberville said, "much less four in a game."

*Ronnie Brown set the tone against Tennessee by running
over Jason Allen on his way to the end zone.*
Ray Cobb/Icon SMI

JASON, MEET RONNIE

While Rosegreen gave the Tennessee quarterback fits, tailback
Ronnie Brown delivered a blow that hurt Tennessee's confidence as
much as it hurt safety Jason Allen's head—as well as his pride.

With Auburn facing second and goal at the Tennessee line and the
score still tied at 0-0, Brown replaced Carnell Williams, took a handoff,
ran off right tackle and found Allen waiting for him near the goal line.
When Allen came up to meet him, Brown lowered his head and shoulders into a battering ram and slammed Allen to the turf. Allen's helmet
flew off as Brown rushed into the end zone for a touchdown.

"The offense came out all pumped up and excited, and I was on the
sidelines resting up. I had come out a couple of plays earlier for Carnell,
and then Carnell came out and I was ready to go," Brown said.
"Emotions were high, and the offensive line did a great job getting me
into the secondary. From then on it's my job to get into the end zone.

"All I saw was the end zone, and there was just one man between me and the end zone. I pretty much felt like I had the advantage, especially with my size and him being a defensive back.

"I really didn't think too much about running around him, so I headed straight for the end zone. He saw me coming through the hole and he broke down and I think maybe he was waiting for me to make a move, but I was just thinking about getting into the end zone any way possible, and the shortest distance between me and the end zone was through him."

Brown never even saw Allen or his helmet rolling on the ground because he was too busy getting mobbed by his teammates and returning to the Auburn sideline.

"I just got up and went to the sideline," Brown said. "I got on the bus after the game, checked my messages and somebody had called and said I knocked his helmet off. I was like, 'For real?' I didn't even see it. It was a surprise to me."

The touchdown run also appeared to surprise Tennessee players, because it seemed to take something out of the Vols at that point. Either way, Brown's score had given the Tigers an early confidence boost.

"I really felt like it elevated our intensity as a team," Brown said. "We scored on that play and then the defense and the specials elevated their play and then it sort of snowballed."

LESSONS LEARNED

Brown's touchdown, combined with Auburn's first-half performance, taught the Tigers some valuable lessons that day.

First of all, the Tigers came to see and believe all Borges had told them about his offensive scheme and their own ability to succeed in it.

"A lot of people make the mistake of thinking since we're a West Coast offense we must be a finesse offense," Brown said, "but our game ever since I've been here at Auburn has been power football, and that really didn't change when Coach Borges came in. We still ran the ball. We just ran a few more pass plays and executed better. But when it came time to get down and get ready to go, everyone knew we could get physical and run the ball, especially the offensive linemen."

In the process, the Tigers also learned something about themselves both as individuals and a collective unit—something that would carry over to the rest of the season.

"As a strength coach I look for a couple of things during a game," strength and conditioning coach Kevin Yoxall said. "I feel like my staff and I have done well if we're physically dominant, not only on both sides of the line, but if our other positional players are physically dominant as well. We had a lot of performances like that that night, like Ronnie Brown scoring by just bowling over a defensive back and the kid's helmet popping off.

"Ronnie's a big physical kid anyway, and he can do some things in here [the weight room] that will make your jaw drop a little bit. There were times when he would just stiff-arm a guy and knock him down, but that touchdown was very impressive.

"We matched up with Tennessee so well, and that made me very proud."

HALF IS ENOUGH

By the time the Tigers were done delivering their first-half message to Tennessee, they were ahead 31-3, and the game was well in hand.

"We knew it was very important, coming on the road, that you have to get off to a fast start," Campbell said. "Coming into a place like Tennessee, with 110,000, we knew it was going to be really loud. The main thing we wanted to do offensively and defensively was to try and make some plays and get their crowd out of the game."

After a hushed gloom fell over Neyland Stadium in the first half, Vol fans took turns making an early departure throughout the second half as Auburn pushed and shoved its way to a 34-10 victory that surprised even the Tigers themselves.

"We never expected this," Carnell Williams said after the game. "It was overwhelming. We just came out and played one heck of a football game tonight. Last year we had never dealt with hype like we had, but this year we're more prepared. You can't worry about the rankings and things like that. You have to go and prove it."

The Tigers proved enough that night to climb to No. 6 in the national polls, but nothing, not even headlines such as "Does Auburn Dream of a National Title" in the *Birmingham News*, could get them to look too far into the future at that point.

"After we beat Tennessee in Tennessee and blew them out in the first half and beat them so convincingly, we knew something special was happening," Aromashodu said. "That's probably the first time we started thinking about the national championship, but nobody really said it."

CHAPTER 11

The Secondary: Mr. Rogers's Neighborhood

Carlos Rogers has always been a confident athlete, at his best when he's locked in man-to-man coverage with a receiver in the open field between the hash marks and the boundary. At the ESPN College Football Awards Show in Orlando, however, he was out of his element, surrounded by uncertainty and worthy award candidates, unable to control the situation.

Surely the Jim Thorpe Award would go to Antrel Rolle of Miami or Ernest Shazor of Michigan. Rogers knew, just knew, his name would not be called.

"I really didn't think it would be," Rogers confessed. "I thought it was going to be Antrel. I had no idea."

All he could do was sit by associate media relations director Kirk Sampson and wait to get it all over with so he could return home to Auburn and start preparing for the Sugar Bowl.

"At first I was just nervous," Rogers said. "I was sitting next to Kirk and I had a program in my hands and he said, 'Let me take your program in case they call you.' I told him, 'Don't worry. They aren't going to call me anyway.'

"My heart was beating real hard and I was so scared, and then they called my name."

At first, Rogers found himself more surprised and relieved than happy to be selected as the nation's top defensive back after allowing only 18 pass completions all season and playing a key factor in Auburn's run defense and special teams in 2004.

The joy, Rogers figured, would come someday when he could just sit back and think about it. He figured wrong, because back at Auburn his coaches and teammates were celebrating an award they insisted he deserved all along.

"I'd watched him on film," said defensive coordinator Gene Chizik, reflecting back on when he arrived at Auburn in 2002 and inherited Rogers as a sophomore. "When I watched him on film the year he played as a true freshman, I knew he could be special. God blessed him with a lot of ability and talent. What we've been trying to do is cultivate that and make it rise to the top. We kept working and working, knowing in the end good things would happen for him. You couldn't have scripted it any better."

THE RIGHT DECISION

After starting 31 of his first 37 games at Auburn and seeing his interceptions fall from four as a sophomore to only one as a junior, Rogers worried that NFL scouts and the media might think he had taken a step in the wrong direction in 2003. The statistical drop wasn't all his fault, though. Instead, he had done such an effective job in one-on-one coverage that teams simply stopped throwing in his direction. Despite that fact, he completed his junior season with little notoriety and a decision to make about his senior season.

"Before my senior year I never felt like I got the recognition or the publicity I should have gotten," Rogers said.

Part of him wanted to return to Auburn for his senior season and prove his point. Another part of him wanted to take his chances and enter the NFL draft.

"My family helped me see both sides of it, and then they put in my hands and told me to make the best decision for me," Rogers said. "Coach Chizik and Coach Tubs gave me both sides, too, but they showed me my opportunities for my senior season, too."

When it came time to make a decision Rogers joined with tailbacks Carnell Williams and Ronnie Brown and announced his plan to return to Auburn for one more season.

"I wanted to come back and be recognized as one of the top DBs in the nation," Rogers said. "Plus I knew either Carnell or Ronnie would probably come back, so I knew we'd have a good running game and I knew Jason [Campbell] was going to get better, and I knew the defense was young but talented and we could do something special here. I knew we had a lot of young guys who needed a leader, someone who could show them things."

That leadership turned out to be a vital factor in Auburn's defensive success, especially when the Tigers lost potential starting cornerback David Irons to a season-ending knee injury early in the preseason, forcing sophomore Montavis Pitts into the starting lineup ahead of schedule.

"I don't like to think about what would have happened without Carlos," linebacker Travis Williams said. "If you look at the whole scenario, what if he hadn't come back and then David Irons got hurt in two-a-days and then Montae [Pitts] was kind of young at the start of the season, so we'd probably have had to put a freshman or someone who wasn't ready at the other corner. Things happen for a reason, and we're so glad he came back."

When Rogers looks back he feels the same way about his decision. Playing a critical role for a 13-0 team and winning a national award will do that.

"I was always pretty comfortable with my choice when I decided to come back," Rogers said, "but you could see the work ethic coming together during the summer, and in the first few weeks of the season everything started going good for us, I thought it was a really good decision. Then to go undefeated and win the SEC and be up for so many awards and win these awards, to be recognized as the best defensive back in the nation, that really made it special."

LONELY EXISTENCE

While it took a while for Rogers's name to find its way to the national college football landscape, his teammates became convinced of his value early on.

"Carlos is a lock-down corner who can play a whole half of the field by himself," linebacker Travis Williams said. "There were a lot of times in meetings when Coach Chizik would say, 'OK, Carlos you've got that man by yourself, no help,' and that's a big deal for a D-coordinator to say that you've got a man one-on-one, by yourself, no help. But the more games we played, the more confidence he had in himself and the scheme, and that's big.

"No one would throw at him—that's respect. Teams see that on film and they know they won't throw at him, either. They're seeing, 'Hey, they're not throwing near 14, so he must be good.' Winning the Thorpe Award was huge, but man, he deserved it."

Opposing coaches and quarterbacks saw the same thing, so they stopped challenging him on a regular basis during his junior season. While that led to fewer interceptions and considerable frustration for Rogers, it eventually became a source of pride for Rogers. Of the 329 passes opponents threw against Auburn in 2004, only 65 (20 percent) were thrown in his general direction. Most of the passes caught in front of Rogers came when he was instructed to play cautious zone defense.

"In last year's games I was so bored, because a lot of times I wasn't getting any balls thrown my way," Rogers said of the 2003 season. "The quarterbacks would just turn and look the other way. Sometimes I'd even sit back there and leave my man open just a little bit so he might just throw it over my way."

Rogers admitted he often found himself putting ideas in receivers' heads as they returned to the offensive huddle, suggesting that the receivers go back and tell the quarterback they were open and they needed the ball. At times he would bait quarterbacks, pretending he was beat only to use his tremendous make-up speed to come back and make the play.

At other times Rogers would drop back into the secondary, throw his hands up in the air, wave his arms around and point in his direction in the middle of a pass play, hoping he would catch the quarterback's attention and provoke a pass in his general direction.

His tricks rarely worked, so he learned to deal with the lack of attention by turning his own attention toward making himself a better all-around player and enjoying the fruits of a successful season.

"Last year it was frustrating, but this year it wasn't frustrating because I've learned to be more supportive against the run and be more active so I can make other plays," Rogers said. "Playing on special teams was big for me. It kept me out on the field more.

Quarterbacks rarely threw in his direction, but Carlos Rogers
still intercepted two passes.
Photo by Todd J. Van Emst

"They still didn't throw it much in my direction, but when they did I tried to make them pay for it. It was frustrating at times but this year I just got so excited about the way the season was going, I didn't have time to complain about quarterbacks not throwing the ball my way."

Jason Campbell understood. Campbell may have been one of the nation's top quarterbacks in 2004, but he wouldn't have tested Rogers very often, either.

"I've thrown against some great corners, and he's No. 1," Campbell said. "It's just the way he recovers. His recovery speed is so fast. I don't think a lot of people realize that when we're running 40s, but he's just got so much agility and quickness and he puts all that together."

Secondary Concerns

For all Rogers brought to Auburn, especially with his ability to cover half the field, he got plenty of help from the rest of a secondary that emerged as a strength over the course of the 2004 season.

While senior Junior Rosegreen brought plenty of experience and toughness to the secondary, he also brought a degree of doubt into the spring, simply because he had spent so much of his career moving around throughout the defensive backfield.

The emergence of free safety Will Herring as a redshirt freshman in 2003 and throughout the next spring gave the Tigers a solid choice in the middle of the defense. Even though Herring didn't exactly develop into an All-SEC-caliber player, the Opelika High graduate did start 24 consecutive games and finish second on the team with 61 total tackles in 2004.

More important, Herring's play at free safety allowed Rosegreen to make the most of his talents and help the team at strong safety, where Rosegreen led the Tigers with six interceptions, finished third on the team with 57 tackles and earned first-team All-SEC honors from both the coaches and The Associated Press.

"Being a key part of this football team is important to him, and seeing this team be successful is important to him," Auburn coach Tommy Tuberville said midway through the 2004 season. "Junior is a great leader for us. Nobody is going to outwork Junior Rosegreen."

THE WEAKEST LINK?

If a chain is only as strong as its weakest link, then Pitts, both at his best and worst, ultimately defined the secondary.

Auburn coaches had been excited about Pitts's potential ever since he ran a 4.29-second time in the 40-yard dash at the Capital City Combine in the Cramton Bowl in the spring of 2001. He signed with Auburn in 2002 and spent his first season redshirting and working through the challenging transition from playing quarterback at little Loachapoka High to college cornerback.

Pitts spent most of his 2003 season playing special teams and started the Music City Bowl, but the coaches still saw him as a likely back-up to Irons when the Tigers opened preseason practice in 2004. All that changed when Irons went down with his injury and Courtney Denson left the program so he could play quarterback at South Florida. Those losses thrust Pitts into the starting lineup as the defensive back most teams would likely pick on.

At the time, Chizik simply said, "It will be interesting to see what happens at that position." Nine games later, after some uneven performances by Pitts, Chizik had changed his tune to an ominous lament.

"We're just not playing real good in the secondary right now— that's the bottom line," Chizik said before the Georgia game. "That corner position is letting down the whole football team. Right now I don't have any confidence with any other corner we've got in the house other than one. We've got to find a way to get it done."

Chizik turned up the heat under Pitts by giving junior Kevin Hobbs and redshirt freshmen Zach Gilbert and Patrick Lee a chance to compete for more playing time. At first, Pitts turned inward and defensive in the face of Chizik's criticism.

"Sometimes it's 'Why are you talking to me? The older guys are making the same mistakes,'" Pitts said. "It's kind of ticked me off."

It took time and help from those older guys to help Pitts understand Chizik's methods.

"It's a job," Rogers said. "It's a business out there. We're trying to get something done. Coach Chizik has been hard on us ever since we got here—things like giving up deep balls and not stepping up on the run. . . . [Pitts] hasn't been doing the job Coach Chizik thinks he can do. So he's been getting on him a lot. I still think he will end up starting. He just needs to step up and play Montae ball."

"Carlos has that cockiness that corners need," Rosegreen added. "That's what Montae needs. He doesn't have it right now."

SECONDARY STEPS UP

Two weeks after struggling against Ole Miss and one week after an open date, the secondary played its best game of the season against a Georgia offense led by senior quarterback David Greene and senior receivers Reggie Brown and Fred Gibson.

Greene completed 15 of his 22 passes, but he only passed for 159 yards. Most of his yards and his one touchdown came late in Auburn's 24-6 victory. He also threw one interception in the second quarter when Rogers seemed to come out of nowhere and pick off a pass in the end zone with Auburn leading 7-0 and Georgia driving.

Just as important, Pitts also did his part as Auburn held Brown to four catches, 62 yards and no touchdowns and held Gibson without a reception on five passes in his direction.

"That was the big game for us in the secondary," Rogers said. "It's already a big game for a lot of guys on the team but it was even bigger for us because of their receivers and some of the problems we had against Ole Miss. Coach Chizik was giving Montavis a bunch of heat and I was telling him, 'Stop worrying and go out there and get better.'

"We really stepped up. Everybody stepped up, the whole team, but the secondary stepped up. Montavis stepped up, too. He didn't let all that talk get him down. He finally used it to get better and prove he can play in the SEC."

PUMMEL AND PRAY

Rosegreen produced one of the season's most dramatic—and dangerous—plays when he met Georgia's Brown at the intersection of Smack and Down streets.

"We were in cover three and I was rolling to the middle of the field and I was reading David Greene and he was looking to one side the whole time," Rosegreen said. "When you're the last safety and you're playing in the middle of the field you're reading the whole field, and I knew I didn't have any threats coming from the other side of the field because Carlos was on that side, and I knew they were probably going to try Montae.

"Montae was right on [Reggie Brown] but when I saw the receiver break to the ball, I broke to the ball as soon as he broke and he got the ball at a good time. I was trying to make sure he didn't catch the ball. I was trying to separate him from the ball, and that's what I did."

As Brown tumbled to the grass and Herring scooped up the loose ball, Rosegreen jumped to celebrate his jarring hit.

"When you get a monster hit like that, you just lose it," Rosegreen said, "and that's what he did. I've just got so much passion and love for the game and I show it."

Rosegreen's celebration ended as soon as he saw Brown still on the ground, lying limp and motionless. At that point, the Auburn players went to their knees, bowed their heads and began to pray for Brown. It wasn't long before a hushed Jordan-Hare crowd began chanting Brown's name as he left the field.

"We're a humble team and we don't wish any bad on anybody," Rosegreen said. "We're trying to win the game, and we want to do whatever it takes, but at the same time, whether it's one of our players or their players, we're going to get down on our knees and pray."

But not until the whistle has blown and the play is over.

"When you get a chance to make a big play, you've got to make it," Rosegreen said, "and that's what I did."

CHAPTER 12

Louisiana Tech: 'A Complete Team'

With the victory at Tennessee, Auburn's seventh consecutive win and its fifth of the season, the Tigers moved up to No. 6 in both polls and immediately stepped into a precarious position.

Despite the fact that it was only the second week of October and the schedule still included six more opponents, the Tigers suddenly found themselves in the thick of national championship discussions initiated by media and fans. From ESPN to newspapers, radio call-in shows and message boards, the Tigers were now being mentioned in the same sentence with USC, Oklahoma and Miami.

Meanwhile, back in Auburn, the Tigers tried to tighten their blinders and keep their focus straight ahead.

"We don't talk about any kind of scenarios—we want our guys concentrating on next week and taking it one at a time," head coach Tommy Tuberville said. "We have a good senior leadership group that understands this thing can turn on you in a matter of days."

Besides, Tuberville added, "We can be much better than we've played. It's not like we've peaked by any stretch of imagination."

With all the talk about SEC and national championships, it almost seemed as if Auburn's next opponent, Louisiana Tech, would have disappeared from the radar if it had not been for the coaching staff and those senior leaders, including quarterback Jason Campbell.

"In our team meeting on Sunday, Jason got up and said some good words," wide receiver Courtney Taylor said. "He said, 'It's not over with. We need to focus. Don't let everybody pat you on the back or anything.'

"A lot of guys are stepping up. There's a lot more vocal leadership going on now."

WRECK TECH

That leadership was evident in the Louisiana Tech game. When Tech focused its defensive effort on stopping Carnell Williams, Ronnie Brown crashed through the Bulldog defense for 109 yards on just 10 carries and Campbell completed 13 of 18 passes for 201 yards and two touchdowns.

With the defense holding Tech to 222 total yards and adding a touchdown on Carlos Rogers's 53-yard interception return, the Tigers led 24-0 at halftime and never looked back on their way to a 52-7 victory.

While Tuberville was the first to admit it wasn't Auburn at its best, saying "It wasn't a rah-rah game," he also followed with a good point about the Tigers' workmanlike performance.

"You can't continue to get them to the top each week mentally," Tuberville said. "If you do, they'll burn out before the end of the season."

Even though they didn't see Auburn's best that day, the Bulldogs were impressed with what they did see from the Tigers.

"No doubt in my mind this team has a legitimate shot at the national championship," Tech quarterback Matt Kubik said. "They have a national championship-caliber defense."

That opinion wouldn't have meant much if the Bulldogs had not already played three top-10 teams at that point in the season.

"They're all good, but I have to say Auburn, to me, is a very complete team," Louisiana Tech coach Jack Bicknell III said. "They have great receivers, a great quarterback, great running backs, a great offensive line and a great defense. That's a complete team all around."

KNOW YOUR ROLE·

Bicknell would get no argument from Williams. He had to fight for 56 yards on 12 carries against Tech but came away from the game more than satisfied with the day. It was a team-first attitude that became more and more pervasive throughout the team with every week and every victory, but when it came from the star running back, it meant so much more.

"I can think back to a time when I was doing good, rushing good, but we were still losing," Williams said. "Now I'm not doing as good—not doing bad, just not doing as good—but we're 6-0.

"The atmosphere is crazy around here. The buzz, the chemistry we have on this team, I wouldn't trade it for anything in the world."

CHAPTER 13

The Defensive Line: Old Hands and Young Pups

It's amazing how a position that became such a strength in 2004 started out as such a concern for Auburn. With the loss of starters Reggie Torbor, Spencer Johnson and DeMarco McNeil from the 2003 defensive line, assistant coaches Terry Price and Don Dunn found themselves starting over with a group of experienced-but-anonymous seniors and several talented-but-unproven younger players.

With so many questions to answer, Price and Dunn went about pushing, prodding and pulling the younger players to provide those answers in the spring and preseason.

"Some of them weren't quite so enthusiastic during two-a-days," Price said. "I pushed those guys as hard as I've ever pushed a group during two-a-days, because I knew we were going to have to have a lot of those young guys help our team.

"I've always believed if you don't push someone to their limits you'll never know what their limit is, and they'll never know what their limit is. If you push these guys when everything's really not on the line, you'll have a better idea of what they can do when it is on the line and they can get after it and make some things happen."

While the younger defensive linemen saw most of the practice reps, some of the older players found themselves playing the role of player/coach, teaching whenever possible and keeping players in line when necessary.

"It would get boring sometimes, sitting there watching all the young guys learn something because I already knew it, but sometimes I'd realize I was making the same mistake," senior defensive end Bret Eddins said. "I was trying to help those young guys out, but they came along a lot faster than I ever did."

In the process, Eddins learned some valuable lessons he can use later in life, especially when he has teenagers.

"I told Coach Price I can see why he gets so frustrated," Eddins said. "I'm surprised he's still here. I sure don't envy anybody's parents."

Those seniors served as a foundation for the younger players to build on. Without them, who knows where Price and Dunn would have been with the defensive line in 2004.

"I've been with Bret five years and he helped keep me sane," Price said. "It's tough enough getting two young guys ready, but getting four or five young guys ready to play at one time, that'll test your patience. They had to be broke like horses. Those guys were as wild as the day is long, but they've gone through the ringer."

MAKING THE MOVE

The seniors also provided an active example when it came time for the coaches to make some position changes. When spring practice opened, Eddins, Doug Langenfeld and Jay Ratliff all lined up at strong-side end. Before the spring ended, Ratliff moved to tackle.

"Jay didn't want to do it at first, but he didn't want to be selfish, and he was willing to do what was best for the team," Langenfeld said.

Ratliff wasn't much of a talker, but he emerged as a leader by example for Auburn's tackles and nose tackles.

"When they told me he was going to move, I didn't think it was a natural move for him," Eddins said. "But I knew Jay was one of those people who's going to suck it up and make the most of it."

Even with Ratliff at tackle, Eddins and Langenfeld still found themselves sharing time at strongside end with redshirt freshman Quentin Groves when spring practice came to a close, while untested sophomores Stanley McClover and Marquies Gunn shared the weakside end position.

When Price called Langenfeld and asked him if he was willing to move to the opposite end, Langenfeld knew what he had to do.

"I didn't want to be selfish, either," Langenfeld said, "and with me and Bret being experienced guys, I knew it was the best thing for me to play the other end while Stanley, Q [Groves] and Gunn and [sophomore Christopher] Browder could grow into their roles and come in and give us some help and be productive for 10-12-15 plays or so."

For seniors who have paid the price, put their time in and earned their playing time, it can be difficult to sacrifice a position or role for the team.

"You can't play the whole game—we're not video game guys," Langenfeld said. "We knew there were a lot of things Stanley, Q and Browder could do, and they needed to be on the field. We knew we could be better as a group if Bret and I could stay fresh and give those guys a chance to show what they could do."

THE YOUNG AND THE RESTLESS

For all those moves to work, those young guys needed to grow up in a hurry and prepare themselves for life in the SEC. That was especially true of McClover and Groves, the two players with the most potential to become standouts if they would just pay the price.

It didn't help that neither player truly understood his role with the team when preseason practice began. While the older players knew where they stood, McClover and Groves spent so much time fighting for playing time they often wasted their time and energy fighting each other.

"We were at each other's neck. We were vying for that spot," Groves said. "[Price] sat us down and explained that we all have a role to play. He said we either could help or go home."

After sitting out the 2003 season as a partial qualifier and spending all of his time practicing with the scout squad, McClover emerged as one of the best surprises of the spring. He even started the first two games of the season before his inconsistent performance and effort, especially against the run, dropped him out of the starting lineup and into a rotation with Langenfeld and Groves.

No one on the line struggled with his new role more than Groves, who came to Auburn as an undersized 240-pound defensive end, moved to linebacker and spent his freshman season and first spring struggling to learn the new position, only to be moved back to the line during the spring. His frustration with the moves and the demands of

Bret Eddins was one of three seniors who led the
way for Auburn's young defensive linemen.
Photo by Todd J. Van Emst

the coaches reached a peak when he came dangerously close to quitting
during a preseason practice.

"It was like 90, 95 degrees and we were doing pass rush drills, and
my coaches started getting on my back, telling me to do this and telling

me to do that, and to tell you the truth, I just didn't feel like doing it anymore," Groves said. "I went in again and I got blocked real bad and they told me to do it again, and this was like my fourth time in a row, and I was so tired and I just got mad, threw my helmet off and said, 'Forget it.'"

Before Groves could get too far, "the whole defensive line came over and talked to me. They were telling me, 'Man, we need you this year. You can't quit. There's no way around it. You can try and leave but we aren't going to let you.' And they meant it.

"I really heard them when they said, 'We really need you.' I thought of that whenever I went out on the field for the rest of the season. I knew I couldn't let the man beside me down. He's not going to let me down, and I can't let him down."

When Groves returned he reinforced the opinions of his coaches and players about the kind of person and player he would become for the Tigers.

"I pushed them and I pushed them and I pushed them in two-a-days, and a couple of times those guys wanted to walk off the field and quit," Price said. "Quinton Groves did quit at one point, but he came back before the end of practice and got back in the drills. That was really a turning point in his career. Since that point when he walked off the field and walked back on, he's been working on making himself the player he is now."

DIGGING DEEP

Over the course of time the coaches learned how to make the best possible use of each lineman's unique talents. That meant McClover and Groves often got replaced by Langenfeld and Eddins in obvious pass rush situations. They responded by tying for the team lead and finishing third in the SEC with 7.5 sacks each. With Gunn and Langenfeld recording three sacks each and Eddins and Browder and junior tackle nose tackle Tommy Jackson making two sacks each, the Tigers finished third in the SEC with 36 sacks.

"We had so many guys helping us who didn't even play the year before," Langenfeld said. "Marquies Gunn gave up his redshirt year last year because we were lacking depth and he didn't play a lot, but this year he really came on and turned into a real reliable backup. Christopher

Browder really struggled at the first of camp, but he came along slowly, and he's going to be a real good player here."

With interior linemen such as Ratliff, Jackson, junior Wayne Dickens and redshirt freshman Josh Thompson holding their ground in the middle, the Tigers also finished second in the SEC by allowing only 104.2 rushing yards per game.

While the spotlight often shined on McClover and Groves, the real story behind Auburn's success up front was the willingness and ability of 10 players to share four spots on a defense that led the SEC by allowing only 11.3 points per game.

"It's been a unique situation because we've been very top-heavy with fourth- and fifth-year seniors and then a bunch of new guys," Price said. "There's really no in between, so it's been interesting to see how they've mixed together and grown up together and worked together.

"It worked out well, because we had those old hands up there banging heads and the young pups coming out learning from those older guys and making the most of their chance when they got their chance.

"It doesn't matter who starts, who's second team and who's third team. They've done a great job not worrying about who starts. When it's their time to shine, they just go out there and play hard. It's really worked out well."

CROSSING THE LINE

For all the attention focused on McClover and Groves, it was the veterans who held down the front early in the season and put the line on the right track.

"We went into the Mississippi State game not really knowing how good we were and not knowing how good they were," Eddins said. "The way that game went for us was really unfortunate in some ways, because we came out of the game saying, 'We still don't know how good we are or how good they are.'"

The Tigers found out the next week when the defense held LSU scoreless throughout the second half and dominated the line of scrimmage with the game on the line. The defensive front came through in a big way with McClover sacking LSU quarterback Marcus Randall in the third quarter and forcing a fumble that Jackson recovered at the

LSU 42, and with Eddins sacking LSU Randall for a 10-yard loss late in the third quarter.

Eddins later teamed with Jackson for a fourth-quarter sack, but his devastating third-quarter sack became a defining moment for the defensive line. When he came off the line he found nothing but air between Randall and himself, and Eddins immediately wondered if something was wrong.

"You think it's going to be a draw or something bad about to happen when you come that free," Eddins said. "But he kept holding on to it, and I just wanted to keep running and make a big blow when I got there."

The blow was big enough to blow the lid off a concerned Jordan-Hare crowd.

"When Bret got that sack I couldn't hear anything," linebacker Antarrious Thomas said. "It just blew me away. It doesn't get any better than that."

The defensive line did get better after that, improving over the course of the season and giving the entire defense a strong foundation at the point of attack.

"The defensive line is really a big part of what we accomplished," linebacker Travis Williams said. "The linebackers get a lot of the credit because we made a lot of plays and got all the stats, but we wouldn't have made all those plays if it weren't for the D-line doing their job and taking on blockers and letting us do our jobs."

CHAPTER 14

Arkansas: "Auburn Is for Real"

Auburn opened the week before its October 16 home game against Arkansas amidst a headline in the *Birmingham News* that read: "Can Auburn Play for the National Title?"

The season's first Bowl Championship Series rankings would be released the Monday after the Arkansas game, but the fourth-ranked Tigers found themselves focusing on more immediate concerns.

"We've learned a lot from last year, the entire team," head coach Tommy Tuberville said. "We've grown up quite a bit. We haven't talked about polls; haven't worried about them; it really doesn't make a lot of difference. All of that's out of our hands. The only thing in our hands is playing better each week."

Closer to home, the Tigers simply wondered if they could beat an Arkansas team that came to town with a 2-3-1 record at Auburn since joining the SEC and a 2-1 record at Auburn under coach Houston Nutt.

"The higher you move up in the polls, the bigger the bull's-eye gets on your back," nose tackle Tommy Jackson said. "We know where we've come from, we can't overlook anybody. From history, when we play Arkansas it's always a hard-fought game, and that's what we expect."

If the Tigers needed any reminders of past frustrations with Arkansas, they didn't have to look very far.

"They humiliated us, took our manhood, pride and anything else you want to say," said linebackers coach Joe Whitt, referring to Auburn's 38-17 home loss to Arkansas in 2002. "They know. They were here. Preparation is more important than anything we do. The emotional part of the game will take care of itself."

FROM A FLICKER TO A FLAME

The idea was to strike and wound Arkansas quickly. The plan was to go with a flea flicker as soon as possible.

The Tigers had worked on the play all week, with mixed results.

"It worked sometimes, but not as much as we wanted it to," wide receiver Devin Aromashodu said.

Well . . . .

"We only ran it successfully once," wide receiver Courtney Taylor said, "and Devin dropped it."

Yes, but, "We still felt like it could work in the game," Aromashodu said, "so that's why we had it in the game plan for the first series."

Just the thought of it was enough to keep Aromashodu's head spinning the night before.

"I didn't sleep," Aromashodu said. "I was thinking about it the whole time."

The anticipation surrounding the play continued during pregame warmups.

"We'd been practicing this play all week, and before the game our managers and trainers kept asking if we were going to run it," quarterback Jason Campbell said.

When Auburn took possession first and gained a first down with its first two plays, offensive coordinator Al Borges finally pulled the trigger and called the play.

"The guys were so excited to run this play, and I just wanted to keep from overthrowing Devin," Campbell said.

"I was just hoping and praying it would work," Aromashodu said. "I knew if their safety bit on the reverse we could get a touchdown."

With the defense pulled in tight to stop the run, the stage was set for Campbell to pitch the ball to tailback Carnell Williams, who ran to his left and handed the ball off to receiver Courtney Taylor. Moving to his right, Taylor then tossed the ball back to Campbell, who found Aromashodu running free down the sideline. Campbell's pass found its target, and Aromashodu did the rest for a 67-yard touchdown pass and a 7-0 lead one minute, 10 seconds into the game.

OPEN THE FLOODGATES

The Tigers turned their fast start into a 17-0 lead by the end of the first quarter.

"I noticed we had 227 yards of total offense in the first quarter," Tuberville said, "and I thought it was a misprint."

By halftime, the Tigers led 30-7, with tailbacks Ronnie Brown and Carnell Williams teaming up for 97 yards and two carries. By the end of the game, Campbell had completed an astounding 17 of 19 passes for a career-best 297 yards and three touchdowns on the way to a 38-20 victory.

With Borges still pulling new tricks out of his sleeve and the passing game continuing to improve, opponents found themselves facing a different Auburn offense from the one they had seen in 2003.

"We kind of feel like we can't be stopped," Williams said. "If teams are going to keep continuing to crowd the ball, we're going to continue to throw the ball up. I feel like we've got some of the best receivers in the country."

RANK AND FILE

What about one of the best teams in the country? Tuberville wasn't ready to go that far, not after the defense gave up a season-high 332 yards, with too many missed tackles and big pass plays in the second half.

"It's great talk for all our fans," Tuberville said. "Our players and coaches have just locked it out. We're a pretty good football team."

How good? There was no way to know for certain at that point, but with less than 48 hours until the season's first BCS poll, the Tigers were finding it more and more difficult to ignore the national implications of every game.

"Our mission is just to play hard every game and come out and show the world that we're not going to have a letdown this year," strong safety Junior Rosegreen said. "Auburn is for real."

CHAPTER 15

The Wide Receivers: Hands and Hearts

Quarterback Jason Campbell wasn't the only player who took the heat when Auburn struggled to pass the ball effectively through most of the 2003 season. The receivers also caught their share of criticism for not catching enough passes. They were often guilty of missed opportunities and dropped passes, a problem that hit rock bottom when Ben Obomanu dropped a would-be touchdown pass that would have given the Tigers a victory in a 24-20 loss to Ole Miss.

It's easy to forget the fact that Obomanu is an admirable young man who never shied away from his mistake, or the way he set career highs with six receptions and 150 yards that day against Ole Miss, his dramatic 68-yard catch and run for a touchdown to keep Auburn in the game, or even his 51-yard reception that put Auburn in position to win the game in the final minutes.

When outsiders think of Obomanu, they tend to remember that one dropped pass—wide open, in the end zone, at Jordan-Hare Stadium, on national television.

When Auburn coaches and players think of Obomanu, they see beyond one play, one mistake. They see an intelligent person who recorded the team's highest GPA in the spring of 2004. They see a player who never gave up on himself. They see the way he responded to

The improvement of receivers such as Courtney Taylor, left,
and Ben Obomanu opened up Auburn's passing attack.
Grant Halverson/Getty Images

adversity, both that day in 2003 and every day throughout the 2004 season.

"He's got so much character," center Jeremy Ingle said. "He's got so much class, and you know that from the minute you meet him.

"I didn't know what to do after that game. I didn't really want to say anything to him because if I had dropped it I wouldn't have wanted to talk with anybody. I wouldn't have answered [media] questions, I can tell you that."

Instead of dodging the media after the Ole Miss game, Obomanu stayed for every question and offered no excuses for his drop.

"We notice stuff like that," Campbell said. "A guy like that is a guy I want to be throwing the ball to. He's a guy who has heart."

Obomanu went on to answer all the questions about his hands and his heart in 2004 and became one of Auburn's many positive answers to a multitude of preseason questions.

"I think all the guys have learned from that scenario—not what he did but how Ben handled it," head coach Tommy Tuberville said. "He handled it with about as much class as I've ever seen. Players became much closer to Ben after that. Ben's a quiet guy.

"When the other players on the team saw how much Ben was hurting, they brought him under their wings that much more. It was a situation that probably helped this team grow up."

GROWING UP

Perhaps it is appropriate then, that no single group of Auburn players seemed to grow more during the 2004 season than the receivers. While it's easy to point to Campbell's progress as well as the impact of tailbacks Carnell Williams and Ronnie Brown and the improved pass protection by the linemen and backs, it would be foolish to ignore those receivers and tight ends who ran the routes, caught the ball and scored the touchdowns.

"The receivers tend to look better when the quarterback looks better, and he's been able to get them the ball with some consistency," offensive coordinator Al Borges said. "Our quarterback completed about 70 percent of his passes, and a lot of that is because the receivers decided they want to play like they're capable of playing."

One year after the Tigers finished 8-5 and ranked 10th in the SEC in passing offense with 192 passing yards per game and only 10 passing touchdowns, the same receivers played a vital role for a team that finished 13-0 and third in the SEC with 237.4 passing yards per game and 25 touchdown receptions. Williams and Brown did their share of damage in the passing game, but for the most part Campbell and Borges turned to a combination of receivers Courtney Taylor, Devin Aromashodu, Anthony Mix, Silas Daniels and Obomanu and tight ends Cooper Wallace and Cole Bennett.

"We've got a bunch of guys who feel obligated that when they get their opportunity, they've got to do what they've got to do to win games," Borges said. "That's happened for us on offense, defense and specials, but I think what our receivers have done is they've taken the bulls by the horn."

Many of those receivers were forced into playing roles ahead of schedule in 2002 and 2003 because of a lack of productivity and talent among Auburn's older receivers. In 2003, Taylor was a redshirt freshman, while Obomanu, Aromashodu, Mix and Wallace were sophomores thrust into the playing rotation as freshmen in 2002.

By the time 2004 rolled around, they were ready to shed their underachiever label and become playmakers.

"Experience had something to do with it," Borges said. "Some of the kids have gained more confidence with experience, and when you take talented kids and combine a little confidence and experience, you've got a pretty dangerous factor there."

CATCHING ON

Auburn's progress in the passing game did not come without its painful moments, particularly in the Mississippi State game. Mix opened the scoring with a five-yard touchdown catch and later added a 58-yard scoring catch, while Obomanu added touchdown receptions of 25 yards and seven yards, but Campbell completed only eight of 17 passes for 139 yards because the receivers dropped six passes. Aromashodu dropped two passes that appeared to be long completions or potential touchdowns.

"You don't want to say anything negative. You want to be encouraging," Campbell said. "But we need to start catching them. If we drop passes like that against somebody like LSU, it could hurt us really bad."

Challenged by Campbell, their teammates and their coaches throughout the week, the receivers came through in a big way against LSU. No one stood taller than Taylor, who caught two huge passes on Auburn's game-winning drive. "Coach Borges and Coach [Eddie] Gran said, 'C.T., make a play,'" Taylor said. "I said, 'Throw the ball my way, and I'll make a play.'"

One week after going without a reception against Mississippi State, Taylor caught five passes for 71 yards. On a fourth and 12 at the LSU 28 Taylor and Campbell connected for a 14-yard gain. Three plays later on third and 12 at the 16, Taylor and Campbell got together for the decisive touchdown with 1:14 left.

"It couldn't have come at a better time," Taylor said. "The way we won just shows we've got character."

Taylor was talking about his team, but he may as well have been talking about his fellow receivers. Two weeks later the receivers led the way as Auburn jumped out to a 28-point halftime lead at Tennessee, with Campbell throwing a five-yard touchdown pass to Obomanu, setting up a score with a 46-yard completion to Aromashodu, setting up another touchdown with a 31-yard completion to Wallace and connecting with Taylor for a 31-yard scoring pass with 52 seconds left in the half.

"The Tennessee game was a turning point for our receivers with the way they made big plays on the road," Campbell said. "Devin made a big play down the sideline, Courtney caught one and ran for a touchdown. They just made a whole lot of big plays all game.

"After that they knew we were really going to be throwing the ball this year and they got real excited. You could see it in their eyes. They knew you were going to throw the ball and they were going to have an opportunity to make a play, and that got all the receivers pumped up."

The receivers went on to fill the season with memorable plays, with Aromashodu's 67-yard flea-flicker touchdown against Arkansas; a 36-yard pass to Wallace on Auburn's first scoring drive against Ole Miss and another 23-yard reception by Wallace to set up a 21-7 lead; a 29-yard scoring reception by Mix to give Auburn a 14-0 lead against Georgia; a 51-yard pass to Aromashodu that set up Auburn's first touchdown early in the third quarter, followed by a 32-yard touchdown pass to Taylor for a 14-6 lead over Alabama; touchdown passes of 53 yards to Aromashodu and 43 yards to Obomanu in the SEC championship game over Tennessee; Mix catching a 53-yard pass to set up Aromashodu's yard touchdown in the Sugar Bowl against Virginia Tech; and Wallace catching a 35-yard pass to set up another score against Virginia Tech.

"When you're out there working your tail off to get open and you know your quarterback is going to deliver the ball, there's a confidence there, a chemistry," Taylor said. "As the season went on, we got better and better. We just kept progressing game by game."

TAYLOR MADE

No receiver made more plays in 2004 than Taylor, a former high school quarterback from Carrollton, Alabama, who redshirted as a freshman in 2002 and made a positive transition to receiver in 2003, catching at least one pass in every game, starting five games and finishing second on the team with 34 catches for 379 yards.

If he needed any incentive to keep improving, he found it during the summer of 2004 while working at the Wynnsong Theatres in Auburn. Taylor was taking tickets until a walkie-talkie call sent him to the restroom to deal with an overflowing toilet.

"I thought I'd quit that night," Taylor said. "Three hours of mopping up water isn't my way of spending a day. It's weird to think that I was doing that this year. It seems like it was 1999 or something. That's a journey—cleaning toilets to ESPN in a few months."

A few minutes in Taylor's presence is a journey into the comic unknown, simply because Taylor is bound to say anything at any time and find the humor in any situation. Reporters flock to him, teammates love to have him around, and coaches wonder what he'll do next.

"If football doesn't work out or whatever, he has a career in the movies," nose tackle Tommy Jackson said. "The thing that sticks out about his jokes is that he's sharp. You think he's just some regular old dude, but then he'll put stuff together and it's hilarious."

Taylor is more than a comic. He's also a highly competitive, self-motivated player who built on his 2003 progress by earning a starting job in the spring. He struggled early in the 2004 season until his clutch performance in the LSU game, and from that point on he became Campbell's most reliable go-to receiver, starting all 13 games and leading the Tigers with 43 receptions, 737 yards, 17.1 yards per catch and six touchdowns.

"My confidence wavered at times," Taylor said. "I've always been a confident, competitive person, and competition usually brings that out in me, but it wavered at times early in the season. By the end of the season, I was on a high and just rolling."

For all of Taylor's importance to a 13-0 team with the SEC's leading scoring offense, the SEC coaches and The Associated Press voted him no higher than honorable mention all-conference in mid-December. The postseason snub caught Taylor by surprise, but in the long run the conference coaches may have done more harm than good by giving him yet another reason to get better.

"I was so upset so I called my mom, and she said, 'It's OK, you have next year,'" Taylor said. "I hate it when people tell me that. I might not even live until next year."

Stopping to think about what he had just said, Taylor laughed at himself before turning quiet and serious again.

"I'm just too competitive," Taylor said. "I feel like I outplayed most of the guys who won the awards but I also understand a lot of those guys who were voted ahead of me are seniors and they battled, but it still makes me upset every time I think about it.

"But that's life. I'll move on and get better. I'll use that as motivation for the offseason."

CHAPTER 16

Kentucky: Handling the Hype

When the Bowl Championship Series standings made its season debut on October 18, Auburn suddenly found itself in the middle of a national championship tempest at No. 4, right behind USC, Oklahoma and Miami.

It didn't take long for the news to reach Auburn—or its most faithful fans.

"I've already gotten a phone call from my mother talking about the BCS," head coach Tommy Tuberville said that afternoon. "There's going to be a lot of talk about it. Our players are going to be subjected to it on campus, in their apartments, in dorms, in phone calls from home.

"We will not have any talk about it around the office building, in the meeting rooms or on the practice field. But I'm not naive enough to believe it won't be talked about somewhere else, which is fine. That's what it is all about. It should be fun. But we also have to understand how we got here. One loss will pretty much kick us out of it."

That loss wasn't likely to come that week with the Tigers playing host to Kentucky but even a listless, uninspired performance would be enough to hurt Auburn in the national polls and the BCS.

"The BCS standings will take care of itself," said Tuberville, whose Tigers entered the week ranked third in both polls. "But this will give our team a little bit more incentive, a little more exposure going into the next few games and, obviously, a little bit more added pressure. I think we can handle all of that."

SOMETIMES YOU GET WHAT YOU NEED

Just 11 minutes, 13 seconds into the Kentucky game, the Tigers were already searching for some added incentive. After ripping into the Wildcats for two touchdowns by Carnell Williams, a touchdown by Ronnie Brown and a 21-0 first-quarter lead, the Tigers allowed Kentucky to drive 80 yards for a touchdown. Then, instead of responding with another score, the Auburn coaches turned to the bench and replaced the starting offense.

"I was grabbing my helmet and getting ready to go back in and Carnell and Ronnie stopped me," quarterback Jason Campbell said. "They said, 'Where are you going?' I thought I was still in the game. I didn't know. I was surprised."

The surprise continued when backup quarterback Brandon Cox threw an interception and the offense went into a funk that lasted until the second possession of the second half. Fortunately for the offense, the nation's No. 2 scoring defense turned up the heat, sacking Kentucky quarterback Andre Woodson eight times, holding Kentucky to 110 total yards and 37 rushing yards on 36 carries. Five different ends recorded sacks, with redshirt freshman Quentin Groves producing four.

"It started at the hotel last night when Coach [Gene] Chizik was talking about us getting off our blocks," Groves said. "He told us when we were in man that we should always be able to beat our man. I just went out and tried to compete and did what he asked me to do.

"It is a great feeling to be able to continue to win. We know what we have to do when we go out to play, and we did it."

Still, the Tigers were hardly impressed with themselves—starting with Tuberville.

"We came out good and played hard, and then I kind of let the air out of it and we got sloppy," Tuberville said.

On the positive side, the Tigers still won 42-10, emptied the bench and rested the starters during the fourth quarter.

"We pretty much dominated the game," Tuberville said. "The score could have been worse than what it was. But there was no use in it. We needed to play everybody."

TRICK OR TREAT

Even Auburn's mistakes seemed to work out for the best. On his postgame radio show Tuberville joked about bringing Halloween candy to his house for his sons Troy and Tucker, since he had been unable to go out trick-or-treating with them. He even went so far as to share his home address live on the air before he realized his error.

When he arrived home early Sunday morning he found a multitude of candy, snacks and drinks stacked on the family's front porch.

"I didn't think anybody would actually do it," Tuberville said. "My sons were real happy about it, though."

CHAPTER 17
The Linebackers: Old School Heart and Soul

No single person is able to compare the best Auburn teams of the past three decades than linebacker coach Joe Whitt. Others have spent more time around the program in administrative roles, and former coach Pat Dye remains a fixture in and around the athletic department, but Whitt has kept his finger on the pulse of the program since 1981, working for Dye and Terry Bowden and current head coach Tommy Tuberville.

No one has spent more time on the practice field and on the sidelines on game day, immersed in the program's best and worst times over the past 25 years than Whitt. And no one could be more "old school" and less prone to hyperbole than Whitt.

So when Whitt compares Auburn's best teams during his time on The Plains, it's worth paying attention. He's seen them all up close and personal, from the 1983 team that came painfully close to winning the national championships; to the outstanding defenses of the 1987 and 1988 teams; to the 1989 team that beat Alabama in the Crimson Tide's first trip to Auburn; to the 1993 team that emerged from the depths of scandal and probation to finish 11-0 in Bowden's first season.

"They're all good teams, and it's really hard to compare," Whitt said. "I've been fortunate to have been a part of all of those teams, but they're all different. But you've got to say the '83 team, '93 and this team, the 2004 team, they stand apart.

"This team, when you look across the board, has a lot going for it. Look at the offense. You've got a quarterback who was a big-timer coming out, and he's a big-timer now, too. You've got two big-time running backs. Some of the wide receivers were big-timers coming out and they've come around and become pretty good. That's a lot of weapons. The offensive line has a few big names going for it, like Marcus McNeil, but then you have a few guys who weren't really known in recruiting. Our center is a walk-on. Nobody really recruited Danny Lindsey, either.

"Defensively, it's different. Start with the linebackers. Not a big-name guy in the bunch. Travis Williams, nobody really wanted him. He's from Spring Valley, South Carolina, but none of those schools over there offered him. Antarrious Williams wasn't highly recruited. Kevin Sears wasn't highly recruited.

"Then you go to the D-line. Bret Eddins is an Auburn guy. He was recruited by us and a few other people early on. The other end [Doug Langenfeld] is a junior college transfer. Tommy Jackson wasn't highly recruited. Jay Ratliff got some offers, but he wasn't a guy people were knocking the door to get and he started out here as a tight end.

"In the secondary, the corners, Carlos Rogers and Montavis Pitts were fairly highly recruited. At the safeties, Junior Rosegreen was fairly highly recruited, but Will Herring was not real highly recruited. Nobody big offered him but us, and he played early for us.

"My point is that this team on defense probably has more no-names who have made a name than any group I've coached."

In some ways, the 2004 can be compared to a 1989 team that came a long way in one season, overcoming early losses to Tennessee and Florida State to give the program its third consecutive SEC championship and its fourth consecutive victory over Alabama.

"Because defensively we started out the season with everybody not knowing how good we were going to be and we grew into a pretty good team over the course of the season," Whitt said. "The difference is that we lost some games early in that season, to Tennessee and Florida State, before we got things turned around. But by the end of the year we were pretty solid."

In other ways, the 2004 is a lot like the magical 1993 team that entered the season picked to finish at the bottom of the SEC West.

"This team is more like the '93 team than any other," Whitt said. "The '93 team had Stephen Davis, James Bostic, Frankie Sanders, Stan White, Thomas Bailey, Wayne Gandy, Anthony Redmon. That was a talented offense, a lot like this offense.

"But the defense in '93 was a lot like this one. We had a walk-on, Jason Miska, at middle linebacker, and a true freshman, Marcellus Mostella, at one linebacker. Willie Whitehead was at one end, and he started here as a walk-on. The other end was Gary Walker, who's still in the NFL. But the inside guys were Damon Primus and Mike Pelton, who had been a linebacker before he moved to tackle.

"The secondary had Calvin Jackson and Brian Robinson from Fort Lauderdale, but the other guys, Chris Shelling, Fred Smith and Ken Alvis, those guys were not highly recruited. So that defense was a lot like this defense."

Like the 2004 team, the 1993 emerged from adversity and low expectations by growing up together and improving one game at a time.

"That team was hungry, because the year before we were young and we came so close to being better, but we just couldn't get over the hump in so many close games," Whitt said. "Those kids were hungry and they had something to prove because of what happened the year before, and this group was hungry because of what happened the year before.

"This is a good team. I guess the best thing about this team was that it was the epitome of team. It's a very unselfish team, a bunch that truly cares about team."

WORKIN' THE MIKE

No one epitomized Auburn's impressive growth during the 2004 season more than Whitt's linebackers. After losing starters Karlos Dansby and Dontarrious Thomas to the first two rounds of the 2004 NFL Draft, it took a veteran coach to see the possibilities buried beneath the doubts surrounding Auburn's returning linebackers.

It didn't help when the Tigers lost one potential starter in the spring. Middle linebacker Lemarcus Rowell had been arrested and suspended in 2003 and forced to spend the 2003 season at Itawamba Community College, proving he could keep his nose clean and earn his way back onto the team. However, Rowell, a former Parade All-

American who never really bought into the program like so many of the successful players on the 2004 team, quit at the end of spring practice.

That gave Whitt one less player to work with at the middle, or Mike, linebacker position. It also gave him one less problem to worry about.

"We were counting on him. We expected him to be with us in the spring in the middle," Whitt said. "When he didn't come through, we just went back to work to find someone else in the middle."

Despite the return of only one starter, outside linebacker Travis Williams, Whitt remained convinced his combination of linebackers could get the job done.

"I thought back in the spring, to be quite honest with you, that we would be all right—once we got the Mike backer situation settled," Whitt said. "In the beginning we were going to leave Travis at Will along with Antarrious and let them alternate. We were going to be as good as you could get at Will. Then we moved Karibi Dede from safety to Sam linebacker and he had a really nice spring and Kevin Sears had a tremendous spring, so I felt good there.

"We felt like we were pretty solid at those two spots, but the only problem we were having is that I didn't feel like we were solid at Mike. We had three guys working there but none of them jumped out there and locked it down, so we decided after the spring we were going to make a change."

When Rowell left the program, senior Mayo Sowell remained the only senior with experience at middle linebacker.

"I knew Mayo Sowell could be a solid player and start, and if he didn't start, he'd at least be solid, a real team guy," Whitt said. "But we still didn't have a guy like I wanted at the Mike, so we moved Travis there, and that made Antarrious the starter at the Will."

THE SKINNY ON WILLIAMS, PARTS I AND II

The move met with immediate skepticism because of Travis Williams's lack of size at 6-1, 212 pounds. Even in Tuberville's philosophy of speed over size, Williams appeared to be too small to take on blockers in the middle of the defense.

"I never questioned him, but people on the outside questioned his size, whether he'd be able to handle it," Whitt said. "He'll tell you that

Linebackers coach Joe Whitt has seen enough Auburn football to rank the 2004 team among Auburn's best.
Photo by Todd J. Van Emst

because I saw him every day and told him every day. I recruited him, so I know him very well and I knew he was hard-nosed enough to get the job done. He's very, very intelligent, too, and a fun kid to be around."

He also proved to be big enough, tough enough and smart enough to top the Tigers with 80 tackles and emerge as a key team leader in 2004.

"Travis, without question, is the leader of the pack," Whitt said. "He is everything you look for. I know last year and this year they will continue to question his size. But he's a great person and a very good football player.

"His football play, pound for pound, is as good as anybody that's playing the game. He loves the game, studies the game and has a passion for it. And there can't be any better human being in this world."

Like Travis Williams, Antarrious Williams faced many of the same doubts because of his size at 5-11, 210 pounds.

"A lot of people dogged us because of our size," Antarrious Williams said, "but what we lack in size, we make up in speed and heart. If they still have questions, hopefully they've been answered."

Like Travis, Antarrious defied those doubts and emerged as a solid playmaker for the Tigers, finishing with 44 tackles despite missing the last three games of the season with a broken wrist.

"When you think about Antarrious, what a heart," Whitt said. "He's had several different kinds of injuries and could have very easily walked in and said, 'Coach, I'm going to just give it up.' But that's not a thought or an option for him. His only thought is getting better and making Auburn better.

"He's another great person that's very quiet. He's got the right heart and everybody loves him."

DEPTH AND EXPERIENCE

Unlike Williams, Sears brought plenty of size to his job as a 6-4, 244-pound strongside linebacker. He started 12 games in 2004 but actually shared the job with Dede, a 6-1, 215-pound special education major who delivered a special presentation on children with disabilities to education specialists at a professional conference in March 2005.

Together, they combined for 58 tackles and five tackles for losses.

"Karibi Dede is like a starter," Whitt said. "He's a true swing guy. He can play Sam and Will and is very good at it. Karibi gives us a different dimension.

"Karibi brings the talent of a defensive back that has the mentality of a linebacker. He has great speed, quickness and awareness. He can do a lot of things against the passing game, and he's solid against the run.

"Kevin who starts at Sam is a physical strong guy who can play Sam, Mike or Will. He's good in the passing game. But I would have to say Karibi has an edge in the passing game, and Kevin has an edge in the run game. They complement each other quite well."

With seniors Derrick Graves and Sowell serving as backups, Auburn's linebackers brought quality experience and depth to the position. Graves played a key role late in the season when he replaced Antarrious Williams in the starting lineup and made some big plays in big games.

"Derrick Graves has been a big blue-collar worker and a real team guy," Whitt said. "I'm mighty proud of him—both of him and for him."

DIGGING DEEPER

For all those positives, the linebackers still had a lot to prove when the season opened. They faced their toughest test in the third game and held LSU scoreless in the second half of a dramatic 10-9 victory.

"The defense went into that game with a lot of question marks, and LSU came in highly ranked," Whitt said. "Nobody knew how good they were at the time, but nobody knew how good we were, either. We go out there and give up nine quick points, but we hold them without a score in the second half and win the game."

The linebackers also proved themselves in the Ole Miss game by playing through the injuries and fatigue of nine consecutive games without a break to come up with some key stops in the second half. Travis Williams felt so ill earlier in the day that he couldn't eat before the game. At halftime he was so dehydrated he needed fluids delivered intravenously so he could play the second half. He responded by leading the Tigers with 12 tackles and earning the SEC Defensive Player of the Week award.

"Travis is a tough guy," Whitt said. "He wouldn't come out of the game even though he had an IV at halftime. He came back out and said, 'Coach, I can go.' And he did. He didn't just play. He played very well."

SOMETHING SPECIAL

Performances such as those made the 2004 extra special for Whitt, a hard-nosed ball coach who takes great pride when his players call him "old school." He may be a tough guy on the field, but most of his players leave Auburn—and then return to visit—with a genuine respect for Whitt as a coach and as a man.

Whitt's 2004 linebackers fit that same mold.

"Every one of them brought their own personality to the group," Whitt said. "Every one of them was special and they're probably as good a group of linebackers—as a group—as we've ever had play here, probably in the history of the school."

Even with all the accomplished players he's coached over the years and the championship seasons he's been a part of, the 2004 team will always hold a special place in Whitt's heart.

"I appreciate the kids so much, because it's not about me—it's about them," Whitt said. "They're the most important part of this team and this group in particular was so special, and will always be special to me."

CHAPTER 18

Ole Miss: Something Special Going On

With eight regular-season games down and three to go, Auburn entered the ninth week facing two other opponents in addition to the Ole Miss Rebels and two other more underlying opponents.

First, the Tigers seemed to finally come to the realization that the odds of advancing in the Bowl Championship Series might be even more difficult than they first appeared to be.

Ranked No. 3 in the AP poll, No. 4 in the coaches poll and No. 4 in the BCS, the Tigers couldn't help but look ahead and take stock of the challenge they faced: What if USC, Oklahoma and Miami all remained undefeated through the end of the regular season? Where would that leave the Tigers?

"I'd be shocked if a team ever goes through their schedule in the SEC, wins the SEC championship game, goes 12-0 and does not have the opportunity to win the national championship," head coach Tommy Tuberville said. "It usually works itself out. I'd say there would be something wrong with the system if that happened."

In addition to the national championship system, the Tigers finally hit a wall of sorts with their ninth consecutive game without an open date. If they could just fight through weary legs and nagging injuries one more week they could use the open date the next week to rest, heal and prepare for decisive games against Georgia and Alabama.

In public the coaches put on a positive face, but behind the scenes they worried about their players squeezing out one more victory on the road against Ole Miss.

"Normally this time of year, you feel like your guys would be mentally and physically drained, but that's not what's going on with this team this week," Tuberville told the media. "They are fired up about playing and they are looking forward to this game."

Looking back, strength coach Kevin Yoxall said, "We hit that ninth straight game and fatigue sort of set in, and all we could do was just work through it."

99 STEPS

If the first three quarters of the Ole Miss game provided any indication, the coaches had reason to be concerned. Auburn didn't look as fresh and sharp as it had in previous games and didn't score in the first quarter for the first time all season.

After taking his game to a higher level throughout the season, quarterback Jason Campbell finally struggled, overthrowing and underthrowing the kind of passes he had completed all year, even throwing seven consecutive incompletions at one point. In the second quarter, however, the Tigers produced a drive that said almost as much about the offense as the game-winning drive in the LSU game.

With the offense sputtering, the Tigers took possession of the ball at their own one-yard line and 3:42 left in the first half. At that point Campbell put the offense on his shoulders and completed a 23-yard pass to Courtney Taylor and a 36-yard pass to Cooper Wallace. Ben Obomanu took a reverse seven yards, Carnell Williams ran for six more yards, and Campbell connected with Williams for a 13-yard reception.

Williams rushed for 13 more yards on the next two plays, giving Auburn first and goal at the Ole Miss one-yard line. After an off-side call on Ole Miss put the ball inside the one, offensive coordinator Al Borges didn't need to consult his playbook for the best possible play: send his six-foot-five, 225-pound quarterback behind a tough offensive line for a touchdown and a 7-0 lead with 26 seconds left in the half.

"That drive is something that's going be talked about by our players for a long time," Tuberville said. "We just kept getting better after that."

ON THE DEFENSIVE

The Tigers expanded their lead to 21-7 late in the third quarter, but Ole Miss didn't give up, cutting the lead to 21-14 early in the fourth quarter by taking advantage of Auburn's tired legs and hurting the secondary for some big plays.

Faced with its most difficult test of the season, the defense responded by holding the Rebels to two second-half touchdowns on seven sacks, a third-quarter interception by free safety Will Herring, a third-quarter fumble recovery by linebacker Karibi Dede, and a key three-and-out after Ole Miss trimmed Auburn's lead to seven. No one fought through the exhaustion more than middle linebacker Travis Williams, who overcame pregame illness and halftime dehydration and finished with 12 tackles and a sack on his way to SEC Defensive Player of the Week.

"We were just gassed," Tuberville said. "It seemed like our defense was out there forever."

At the same time, Tuberville added, "We didn't play as good as we've been playing. It says something when you can win on the road in this conference and not play at full strength. We were absolutely running on fumes. At halftime our defense was gassed, but they reached down deep in the second half and played better."

REAPING REWARDS

At the same time, the Tigers got something more than a 35-14 victory out of the game.

"I was telling everybody we need a ballgame like this," Carnell Williams said. "In the past we've been real successful at just jumping on teams and beating them to the punch. We've just kind of taken control of games, but Ole Miss came out ready."

"That was one of those games you need to go through sometimes," Travis Williams added. "To see guys struggle and then fight back like that, that's a good thing."

The Tigers also learned No. 3 Miami had lost earlier in the day to North Carolina. With the Hurricanes falling, the Tigers would be rising in the next BCS standings.

"We just don't want anybody to cheat us. We feel like we're the best team in the nation, and Miami losing means that's one less team to worry about," offensive tackle Marcus McNeil said. "We feel like we can take on the world."

In addition to overcoming their early struggles and improving their national championship stock, the Tigers also clinched the SEC West championship and the program's first trip to Atlanta for the SEC championship game since 2000.

"It's big to get this tonight," Travis Williams said after the game. "In the past we always shared it with someone. Now we can just say that we alone are the Western Division champions."

With so much on the line, the Tigers insist they never panicked when Ole Miss played its way back into the game.

"I wasn't worried—not with this leadership," Carnell Williams said. "With everything we've got going this year, I wasn't worried at all. We've got something special going on.

"It wasn't easy, but we got what we wanted. Where are we going? Atlanta? That's what I like to hear!"

SING A NEW SONG

Williams and his teammates also liked hearing something new in the postgame locker room scene. During the celebration following the win, the Tigers broke with tradition and added another song to their repertoire. In addition to singing the school fight song, "War Eagle," the Tigers created a new tradition by hooking up in the locker room and signing "Hard Fighting Soldier."

From that point on, the song would no longer be reserved for Friday night devotionals. If fans didn't know about the song at this point, they would soon hear it for themselves during the postgame section of Tuberville's weekly television show.

"It's amazing," running backs coach Eddie Gran said. "You get in that locker room and you hook up with each other. You have your arms around the guy next to you. It doesn't matter if he's black, white, red or yellow. You sing that song, and you have 140 of us doing that. It's something you'll never forget."

CHAPTER 19

The Special Teams: Playing to Win

With a 9-0 halftime lead over Virginia Tech in the Sugar Bowl and an outside shot at a national championship still on the line, Auburn assistant coach Eddie Gran decided it was time to pull something new out of Auburn's bag of tricks.

Auburn wouldn't just receive the kickoff to open the second half. The Tigers would run "The Globe." They would catch the kick, gather several players together around the ball, hand the ball to a predetermined player and come flying out, hoping to catch the Hokies by surprise.

It certainly surprised head coach Tommy Tuberville.

"I'm going to be the first to tell you I wasn't for running it," Tuberville said. "Eddie came up to me at halftime and said, 'We're up 9-0, these players have been running this for a month in practice.' I told him, 'I've been watching y'all run it, and it looks like crap to be honest.'

"But Eddie says, 'What do you think of running it at the start of the second half?' Well here we are 12-0 on the season, up 9-0 at halftime and he wants to take Carnell Williams, the SEC Special Teams Player of the Year, have him catch the ball, go to the two-yard line, turn his back to the Virginia Tech players and run a trick play?

"I asked him, 'What if they hit him and he fumbles the ball? Are you going to take the blame? Because if we fumble and they get the ball and win this game, you may just lose your job.'"

Gran refused to back down.

"He looked at me and asked me, 'Do you really want to run this thing?'" Gran said. "I said, 'Yeah, Coach. The kids have practiced it, they're excited about it, they're ready for it.'"

"I finally told him, 'Just make a decision, but don't tell me what you're going to do,'" Tuberville said. "Before the kickoff I just kept my headphones off. I didn't want to know."

Tuberville didn't want to watch, either, but he watched anyway.

Instead of the high kick the Tigers needed to make the play work, they got a line drive, "the worst possible kick," according to Tuberville. That didn't prevent Williams from catching the ball at the goal line. "We got the ball, scattered like a bunch of quail and Carlos Rogers took the ball and ran the ball out to the 22-yard line," Tuberville said.

It wasn't a big return, but it was a positive sign, nonetheless.

"That helped us in that game," Tuberville said. "Our players knew we would do anything we had to do to win the game. We were going to take chances. They know that's our philosophy."

PLAYING THE ODDS

It's a philosophy that originally grew out of desperation. Long before Tuberville earned a national reputation for his willingness to run fake field goals or punts in even the most unusual situations, he decided special teams tricks would help his Ole Miss team survive trying times.

"I got the nickname 'The Riverboat Gambler,' but when we came to Ole Miss we had 52 guys on scholarship and we were on probation and we were awful," Tuberville said. "I took the special teams over and said, 'Guys, we're going to do a lot of different things. We're going to fake field goals, fake punts and do everything we can to try and win a game.' But we had to do things in the special teams to give our team a chance to win."

Tuberville carried that same philosophy to Auburn in 1999, along with Gran as running backs and special teams coach. The Tigers' tendency toward a more conservative special teams approach is in direct correlation to the program's improved talent and depth.

"We've got better football players now, players as good as anyone in the country, but we still try to do different things," Tuberville said. "I can still see it in our guys' eyes when they go to practice and do our special teams, because we try to make it fun. We don't do the same things every week. We're very unorthodox. When you can make plays in the special teams it does more than change the field position. It changes the momentum and gives you a chance to win."

The Tigers played it safer than ever on special teams in 2004, simply because they could afford to.

"Sometimes you run a trick play because you're trying to get better field position and spark something. We didn't have a lot of things we had to get sparked this year," Gran said. "Our offense started out pretty strong, pretty quick, and our kicking game played really well. When you've a defense like that, you really want to play field-position football.

"But our special teams still made a big impact for us. Sometimes your offense sparks you, sometimes it's your defense, but this year, probably more than ever, our kicking game did it for us once in a while."

THE BIGGEST PART

The Tigers took a safer approach in 2004, but they didn't take the special out of special teams. In addition to Williams leading the SEC in all-purpose yards and total punt return yards and earning the SEC Special Teams Player of the Year award, the Tigers played an indisputable role in the team's success.

"It all starts with Coach Tuberville, because the emphasis he puts on special teams makes our jobs as coaches easier," Gran said. "But then our seniors stepped up and really helped make our special teams solid throughout the year. Ronnie Brown, Carnell William, Carlos Rogers, Jay Ratliff, those guys were a big part of our special teams, and they made it important and they made sure the younger guys made it important."

Rogers did his best work on special teams as the gunner on punts, a job that requires the outside players to fight off defenders in an attempt to be the first player downfield to make the tackle and contain the punt returner.

*Punter Kody Bliss was one of many reasons behind
the success of Auburn's special teams.*
Photo by Todd J. Van Emst

"That's one thing I've been doing since I got here, and something I really wanted to do this year," Rogers said. "One of my goals was to really work hard and stand out on special teams and make a difference. People don't realize how much special teams can change a game by giving the defense field position or forcing a turnover.

"A lot of the young guys noticed the way I played special teams and talked to me about it. The same with Ronnie and Carnell. We were out there working hard on special teams trying to make a difference."

Brown did a significant amount of anonymous work in the trenches, including playing along the offensive line on punts and running downfield to make tackles.

"It helped me appreciate the offensive linemen and what they do," Brown said. "The rest of us get all the glory, but it's really those guys who do the dirty work without the glory. Without them we couldn't have gone 13-0 as a team or had any individual success as running backs."

It didn't hurt that all three players improved their NFL draft stock with their willingness and ability to excel on special teams, but all three players took pride in their leadership role on special teams.

"When we sit in our seats for team meetings, the offense sits over on one side and the defense sits over on the other side, but once all of us get together for special teams, we're in the big section in the middle," Rogers said. "That's the biggest part of the game, the special teams."

A Chance to Shine

For players such as Rogers, Brown and Williams, the kicking game can be just another job. For the less famous players who don't see as much playing time at other positions, special teams can be their chance to contribute and shine.

The Tigers had their share of special teams stars in 2004 with players such as junior defensive back Andrew Letts and senior defensive back Donnay Young who didn't see extensive playing time, and players such as wide receiver Anthony Mix and outside linebacker Derrick Graves who were part of the regular playing rotation.

"If you look at guys like Derrick Graves and Donnay Young, those were guys who were three-year starters for us on special teams and gave us everything they had," Gran said.

Between the obvious standouts and the players who made the most of their chance to play a vital role in a 13-0 season, the kicking game truly became special in 2004.

"On every Sunday we'd watch the special teams film as a team—the whole team," Gran said. "You'd have defensive line applauding for a guy running down on kickoffs. You'd have the whole team involved. When somebody did something well, they would clap for that guy. That's a pretty neat feeling for some of those guys I mentioned who are second-team guys and maybe didn't see a lot of playing time, because everyone appreciated their efforts.

"That said a lot about this football team. It was a selfless football team, very much a team in every way."

BIG GAMES, BIG PLAYS

The kicking game made its impact throughout the season, especially in the biggest games. In the LSU game, punter Kody Bliss dropped four punts inside the 20-yard line, and a penalty by LSU allowed kicker Jon Vaughn to make the most of a second chance after he missed a potential game-winning extra point with 1:14 left in the game.

"When I made the kick, I just figured that's the most pressure I could ever experience as a college kicker, making the [PAT] to beat the defending national champions," Vaughn said. "Worrying about making any kick from that point forward would be downhill. I knew I couldn't experience any greater pressure."

In the Tennessee game, the Vols cut Auburn's lead to 31-10 early in the fourth quarter before Devin Aromashodu returned the kickoff 48 yards to the Tennessee 41-yard line, helping Auburn regain the momentum and kick a field goal.

In the Ole Miss game, the Rebels cut Auburn's lead to 21-14 before the defense forced the Rebels out on just three plays and the punt return paved the way for Carnell Williams's 38-yard punt return to the Ole Miss 25 and an Auburn touchdown drive. In that same game Bliss averaged 47.7 yards on six punts and dropped three punts inside the 20, earning SEC Special Teams Player of the Week.

Georgia did block an Auburn punt, but Bliss also dropped two punts inside the 30 and Williams returned four punts for 77 yards against Georgia, setting up a late touchdown with a 40-yard return.

GETTING THEIR KICKS

For the season, Vaughn ended up making 12 of 15 field goals, meeting the preseason goal Gran set for him, and made 51 of 52 PATs. Bliss averaged 42.3 yards per punt and dropped 17 punts inside the 20. Kickoff specialist Phillip Yost sent 43 of his 79 kickoffs for touchbacks.

Not bad for a bunch of kickers.

"I kind of got in trouble before the season when somebody was interviewing me for a story and asked me, 'Is the kicker your teammate all the time, only when he makes a game-winning field goal or none of the time?'" defensive end Bret Eddins said. "If I say, 'Only when he makes a game-winning field goal,' that's as bad as saying 'never,' so I just said 'never,' and I laughed about it. I thought it was a goofy question, so I gave a goofy answer.

"Somebody called my parents and said that was offensive to them, and people got on message boards and said I thought that poorly of the kickers. But I room with Phillip Yost on the road. I was kidding. I'm

CHAPTER 20

The Open Date: Timing Is Everything

Talk about timing. Having survived nine games in nine weeks without a break, Auburn got an open date at the best possible time following the Ole Miss victory.

With the SEC West title already secured, the third-ranked Tigers could finally take some time to rest, heal nagging injuries and prepare for eighth-ranked Georgia.

"We had those nine straight games and then we had a shaky performance against Ole Miss," strength coach Kevin Yoxall said. "But then we had the open date at the best possible time.

"But think back: we beat LSU and then our next opponent [The Citadel] was one we could get through after a big win and let us get ready for the Tennessee game. Then at the end of the regular season we beat our archrival [Alabama] and then we had Thanksgiving week off before we came back and started getting ready for the SEC championship game. There were a lot of opportunities for the kids to recharge themselves and get ready to go again."

PEER PRAISE

The Tigers also needed extra time to deal with the extra media attention that came with their success. The open date became an appropriate time for national and regional media outlets to send reporters to Auburn for feature stories on head coach Tommy Tuberville's comeback and the team's surprising rise through the rankings.

On the SEC coaches' teleconference that week, coaches poured praise on the Tigers with insightful comments.

"I don't think we've played against a team that has played with more grit and tenacity," LSU coach Nick Saban said. "They just hang in there and compete as well as anybody we've played against. They have a great scheme on offense. The two running backs are prime-time players. Jason Campbell has come of age."

Mississippi State coach Sylvester Croom said, "There was something I shared with our team in preparation for our LSU game. There was a point in their LSU game where there was a sideline shot of Auburn. Every person was standing up. They made a play and everyone on that sideline jumped at least three feet in the air.

"Not only is Auburn a talented football team, they have tremendous cohesiveness. They have one mind and one spirit. With the talent they have and the chemistry they have, they are going to be very tough to beat."

PERCEPTION OR REALITY?

The further the Tigers moved into their schedule the more they also came to realize how difficult it would be to move past USC and Oklahoma in the BCS if the Trojans and the Sooners kept winning.

Part of the problem for Auburn was a schedule that included Louisiana-Monroe and The Citadel. Playing The Citadel, a 3-7 Division I-AA team, hurt Auburn's reputation more than it hurt Auburn's reality and it quickly became an easy target for criticism.

In actuality, Auburn originally scheduled Bowling Green, a Mid-American team that went on to finish 8-3 and win the GMAC Bowl. During the spring, however, Oklahoma offered Bowling Green more money than Auburn's original offer of $500,000 to break its contract with Auburn and come to Oklahoma. Auburn countered by offering more than Oklahoma, but Bowling Green athletics director Paul Krebs, a former Oklahoma ticket manager, wanted to play the Sooners.

Unfortunately for Auburn, Bowling Green had to pay only $25,000 to buy its way out of the contract, a stipulation created by former Auburn athletic director Mike Lude when the contract was signed in 1997.

When Auburn sought a replacement it found The Citadel—a game that seemed to be a good fit between the LSU and Tennessee games.

Ultimately, playing The Citadel didn't cost Auburn the national championship. More than anything, the Tigers were hurt by the fact that they started so far back in the polls while USC and Oklahoma started in the top two spots and never lost on the way to the national championship game.

THE STRETCH RUN

For all the talk about the polls and the BCS, the Tigers learned some valuable lessons from their 2003 struggles and their 2004 successes: the only way to get where you want to be is to win one game at a time and concentrate on the things you can control.

Coming out of a productive open date the Tigers had nothing but Georgia on their minds. That was enough for a confident team with its focus intact.

"We don't feel like we have any weaknesses," center Jeremy Ingle said. "It's not cockiness. We've had confidence since the beginning, but now we've actually done the things we thought we could do. We've passed on people, run on people, stopped people. We've done a little bit of everything."

But could they keep doing it against the program's two traditional rivals?

"We have two of our toughest games coming up," Tuberville said. "Not only tough games in the conference, but our two most important games as fans, players and coaches."

CHAPTER 21

The Offensive Line: Putting It on the Line

When Hugh Nall became a convenient lighting rod for criticism of Auburn's offense in 2003, Nall knew head coach Tommy Tuberville had to make a change.

It didn't matter that he had spent the season in an awkward coaching situation, trying to run an offense installed by former coordinator Bobby Petrino with many of the plays being called by first-year quarterbacks coach Steve Ensminger. It didn't matter that he is widely regarded as one of college football's best line coaches, or that the Tigers showed marked improvement in their final two games of the season against Alabama and Wisconsin.

"It was disappointing, as much as you can imagine, knowing that I had finally made some changes that I thought needed to be made that were totally different than the circumstances I had taken the job under," Nall said. "I saw the results of it and thought we had it going in the right direction, but at the same time I knew there was a lot of pressure on Tommy to make a change.

"If it would save everyone's job, that's what I wanted to happen."

While that didn't make a demotion any easier, the situation could have been worse for Nall.

"I pretty much knew it was coming," Nall said. "Tommy called me in and quickly told me that he was going to have to make a change, but he immediately went in to the next phase of it and told me my salary would not change and he wanted me to be there and whoever he hired as offensive coordinator would be somebody I wanted to be hired, somebody I could get along with, or he wasn't going to hire him. Those two things certainly made me feel good about him wanting me to be here."

The actions of both coaches are unusual in the football business.

"Most guys would have called you in to their office and said thanks and that's it," Nall said. "He could have easily fired me or tried to run me off with a reduction in salary or not involving me in whoever we hired. It was really something I appreciate with Tommy, the way he let me know he wanted me to be here."

And most assistant coaches wouldn't have handled it the way Nall did. With his reputation he would have landed a job somewhere sooner than later.

"I believed in our kids. I really felt like we had a bunch of good kids and I thought they'd gotten a bad deal," Nall said. "There were things that didn't take place to give them a whole package.

"Plus I knew I had a chance to have a really good offensive line the next year, and that's something I felt committed to.

"Then the way Tommy put it, that made me want to suck it up and fight through it. And my family likes it here and I didn't want to go through searching for a new job and taking a new job and moving my family.

"I felt like I was man enough to know what I believe in, and I believe in myself and what I can do and I know that what happened [in 2003] really wasn't me. I just decided I'd take it [criticism] and let people think what they're going to think, because they're going to do that anyway."

BRING IN BORGES

Nall also made a total commitment to making the most of his new circumstances, especially when it came to bringing in a new offensive coordinator.

Tuberville had already interviewed several candidates, including two bright young coaching prospects in Toledo's Rob Spence and

Miami of Ohio's Shane Montgomery, and decided he was ready to make a hire when Nall pushed him to dig a little deeper.

"We were running out of time and we were getting closer and closer to spring practice," Nall said, "but I just didn't feel that was the right move, and I appreciate Tommy listening to me, because I felt strongly we should interview at least one more guy—and that guy ended up being Al Borges."

Borges not only brought experience but also a sense of personal security that fit well with the rest of the offensive staff. He wasn't going to be threatened by input or unwilling to change his mind if someone had a better idea.

"The first time I ever visited with Al, I just really got a great feel for him as a good person and for what he wanted to do and how he already had a system in place instead of a developing system," Nall said. "Then he made me feel good in that, basically, I've been in charge of overseeing the running game for about nine years, and he wanted to keep the running game the same.

"It was just a really good meeting as far as feeling like the chemistry was there when we met with Al, and I hadn't felt that way when the other people interviewed."

Borges also told Nall something that put Nall's mind to rest.

"He said, 'I've been a coordinator for 18 or 20 years, and I've made my mistakes. You didn't have a chance to make a mistake,'" Nall said. "That's the way I had always felt about it. I realized he realized the situation and he was willing to work with me, and he knew I was man enough to accept it, and he was the boss and I would have my input, but he would have the final say."

'HE'S MY COACH'

While Nall made the adjustment to his new role and a new offensive coordinator and his offensive linemen came to respect and appreciate Borges, some of Nall's player remained convinced their coach got a raw deal.

Offensive linemen, the anonymous dump trucks and earth movers in a world that salivates over Cadillacs and Escalades, often become a tight-knit group. They fight like brothers, but if you fight one, you'd better be prepared to fight them all. Nall may be a hard-nosed ball

Hugh Nall had a way of being "firmly convincing"
with center Steven Ross and the offensive line.
Photo by Todd J. Van Emst

coach, but some of his players would probably fight to be first in line to take a bullet for him.

"Coach Nall is a great coach, and we were one or two plays away from winning 10 games with him as our offensive coordinator," guard Danny Lindsey said. "I think he deserves another shot to run the offense again at some point, whether it's here or somewhere else. I think he should be a head coach somewhere. He's a great offensive line coach, and he was showing at the end of the [2003] season just how good he could be as a coordinator."

Center Jeremy Ingle added, "Last year was really tough on him. He really enjoyed being the OC, and I really thought he did a good job, to be honest. We were just a play away from winning nine games. There were a lot of people in the Auburn family who were disgruntled about it, but I never really thought he got a fair shake. That's just my opinion, but he's my coach.

"But him going back to just coaching the offensive line and the way he handled it and focused on us daily made us even better and made our whole team better."

BETTER LIVING THROUGH CHEMISTRY

The line came together through a series of key moves by both Nall and the veteran linemen.

The first thing Nall did was stop flipping the line from one side to the other, from strong or tight side to the quick or weak side. He never liked the system in the first place, because he believed it hurt a player's ability to get comfortable in one spot.

His second move was to switch junior Troy Reddick from guard to right tackle, where Reddick became a solid force for the Tigers, especially in the running game.

"The other thing was that I really believed in Jeremy Ingle," Nall said of Ingle, a fifth-year senior who came to Auburn as a walk-on. "I took a lot of flak for the center position. All the experts would always inform me that I had problems at the center position, and I never bought into that.

"I just thought this kid was a special kid. I always knew I had Danny Lindsey to put in there if I needed to, but I really believed in Jeremy and it really paid off. Jeremy Ingle should go down as one of the best centers to have ever played at Auburn."

The line also grew closer over the summer, spending more and time together under the watchful eye of veteran leaders such as Lindsey, Ingle and left tackle Marcus McNeill.

"We all sat down as a group and decided we needed to get closer as a group," Ingle said. "We started doing more things together off the field like going out to eat with each other. By the end of the season we really developed a lot of trust in each other."

They also became experts at finding the best deal for the most food, a skill greatly respected by large men who work and play hard. Often it was chicken wings or nachos, with the guys who could afford to pay sometimes paying for the guys who couldn't. No one made a bigger impact at dinner than sophomore guard Jarrod Britt.

"I've seen him get five or six fish sandwiches and a couple of double cheeseburgers from McDonald's at one time and eat every bit of it. He's slowed down a little bit now, but when he first got here he could really eat," Lindsey said. "When he was a freshman they actually put him on a diet, because he was the only player in the history of the program to ever gain weight during two-a-days. He even got caught trying to take a country fried steak out. He put it up under his armpit because they said he couldn't have any fried food. He's trying to get out of the dining hall with a country fried steak under his armpit and they caught him before he could get out. That's pretty desperate, so yeah, I'd have to say Jarrod is the biggest eater in the group."

Whatever it was that fed the line over the summer, Nall could see something different in the group when the Tigers reported for preseason practice.

"I really started feeling good in two-a-days," Nall said. "I started noticing a chemistry and a mesh I hadn't seen in a long time. As a group their work habits and their attitude were super. You never had anybody late for meetings. You had people trying to be at practice, not trying to be in the training room. They weren't looking for injuries to get out of practice. They were looking for ways to be at practice.

"I knew then if the injury bug didn't bite us too bad this would be a pretty special group."

DEEP THOUGHTS

With McNeill and Reddick at the tackles, Ingle at center, Ben Grubbs and Lindsey at the guards and key backups such as guards Tim Duckworth and Jonathan Palmer, tackles Leon Hart and King Dunlap and center Steven Ross, the Tigers were able to compete for playing time every day. The extra depth gave Nall plenty of leverage in case the older guys started to slip, but he never needed to use it.

"I really thought our two-deep was as good as any I'd been around in terms of potential and ability," Nall said. "The depth created more competition, and that gave me some young guys to push the older guys. If I had had to, I certainly would have put them in, but I didn't have to do that because our older guys weren't worried so much about getting beat out as they were about losing their job. They wanted to be the guy out there on the field, making a difference."

When the injury bug finally made its move and forced Ingle to miss the Ole Miss game with a sprained ankle, Ross stepped in to do an admirable job.

"People have to step up when situations arise, and that's what Steven Ross did against Ole Miss," Nall said. "Once he cleaned out his britches after the first quarter he played better than I would have expected. Unfortunately he got hurt in practice before the championship game, but he's got a bright future ahead of him."

When Ross suffered a season-ending knee injury during the open date, Ingle pushed himself to play through his nagging ankle injury. After Ingle limped off the field in the third quarter of the SEC championship game, Lindsey had to reprise his old role at center, where he had started 13 games in 2003.

"I thought Jeremy was done, so I was shocked when he came back in," Nall said. "I had made the change with Danny going to center and putting Timmy Duckworth in at guard, and the next thing I know Jeremy says he's ready to go back in again. He finished out the game and played well.

"Jeremy knew he had to go back in, and that goes back to the way he and the other guys handled two-a-days, with guys not looking for ways to get out of practice and games but finding ways to get back in."

LEADING THE WAY

For all the attention focused on offensive stars such as Jason Campbell, Ronnie Brown and Carnell Williams, some of the team's most effective and significant leadership came from the offensive line. Ingle became a symbol of that leadership with his climb from walk-on scout team regular to starter.

Ingle actually considered quitting the team at least three times during his time at Auburn. "I didn't know if people even wanted me here," Ingle said. "When you're on the scout team, there's not much love."

If only Ingle had been in the coaching staff's meeting on the Monday morning before the Ole Miss game.

"Ingle had gotten hurt the week before against Kentucky, and in the staff meetings on Monday morning we always talk about the travel squad—who's going to travel, who's not going to travel," Nall said. "In an SEC game only 66 players can travel, and we're going through the list and Tommy gets to Ingle and says, 'Strike Ingle.'

"I said, 'Coach, I think we should travel Jeremy.' He said, 'Why? He's hurt.' And I said, 'Well, I just think he's been a major part of the attitude of this team.' At the end of the meeting I came back to it and said, 'I'm going to stand up and say I think he should travel. I think he's one of the catalysts of this football team. Nobody believed he could get the job done, and he's getting the job done for us.'

"About that time four or five people around the table spoke up and started agreeing, and Coach Tub decided to travel him."

It turned out to be a smart move.

"I have a way of being firmly convincing with Steven, and I have a way of maybe doing that too strong at times," Nall said. "But Jeremy was able to settle him down. After I'd get through with Steven, I'd see Jeremy take over, and that was a big thing for Steven.

"That says a lot about the senior leadership of our offensive line, with Jeremy Ingle, Danny Lindsey and even Rich Trucks. All three of those guys are special, but with Rich, here's a guy who's a walk-on guy, a guy we put on scholarship, but he knew the scholarship would be only a one-year deal and we'd have to have it back after a year, and yet he stuck with it. He's a great guy, a great Auburn man."

PANCAKES FOR EVERYONE

In addition to being a solid, dependable group, the offensive line also provided some of the more unusual moments of the season.

"It was such a focused, dedicated group," Nall said. "When meetings started it was serious business, but some of these guys were pretty loose sometimes. When something funny happens on film that we need to see, like some guy running down the field and tripping like a spastic, we'll run it back three or four times in a meeting. We've got some personalities, but Marcus McNeill is quite a prankster. He keeps the meeting room lively."

McNeill also kept his teammates on their toes, both on and off the field. On the field, McNeill became the team version of Dr. Seuss when it came to dishing out knockdown blocks called "pancakes" in his own unique way, celebrating dominating blocks by yelling out "One cake, two cake, red cake, blue cake."

"After a while people would get pancaked and we'd come up with a name for the pancake or cake they resembled when they got pancaked," McNeill said. "One time it was a double team with Timmy Duckworth and King Dunlap on Josh Thompson and Duck ends up on the bottom and Josh ends up in the middle and King Dunlap ends up on the top, so we called it a 'double-layer chocolate cake with cream in the middle.'

"When Quentin Groves got pancaked, we always called him 'IHOP' for International House of Pancakes, because he's lived all over the place."

McNeill is also a notoriously mischievous storyteller who likes to lure his victims in with wild stories, set the hook and then celebrate his catch with a big "gotcha" grin. His best moment came at a Fellowship of Christian Athletes fundraiser for chaplain Chette Williams's ministry.

"Marcus is one of three of us who has to speak and Marcus gets up there last and starts telling everyone about Chette's ministry," Ingle said. "He starts talking about his first day at Auburn, about going to the store and walking by this liquor store and looking in the window and seeing Chette in there with a gun holding up the liquor store and how Marcus started thinking he had made the wrong decision to come to Auburn.

"You look out at the crowd of about 1,500 people and there's all these people from FCA and all these Christians sitting there quiet with their mouths open, and I'm sitting there thinking, 'What is he talking about?'

"Then all of a sudden he stops and says, 'Aw man, I'm just kidding y'all.' The whole place starts dying laughing. He really had us."

McNeill means no harm. He's just a big kid in a big body. A very big kid in a six-foot-nine, 323-pound body with the potential to make a lot of money in the NFL.

"Me? Not me. I'm very serious," McNeill said with a laugh. "Yeah, I guess I try and have a little fun and make jokes, even in practice. I still take it seriously, but to me it makes practice a much easier thing to be around. If you're serious all the time you're not going to enjoy practice and you're not going to put everything into it."

"This team enjoyed practice because we were out there having fun and laughing and talking trash with the defense and still working hard. Then we'd go out and have dinner and talk about who talked the most trash. The way our team is set up with the people we have, we seem to function better when we're having fun playing football. We have a team that's loose and laidback, not uptight and serious."

TOWING THE LINE

The line also had a way of getting the job done, especially when it had to be done in the big games and the critical situations.

"Hugh Nall is as good if not the best offensive line coach in the country and he proved that this year," Borges said. "We ask them to run block and pass protect and they did both well. They blocked for the run so well that they allowed two great running backs to compile almost 2,000 total yards, and they did such a great job in pass protection that we were able to pass for more than 2,800 yards."

For his part, Nall is quick to praise the linemen who did the dirty work and made the blocks, but he's not getting away that easily. Not as long as his linemen and his peers have something to say.

"I have all the respect in the world for him, and I'm just thankful I got to play for him," Lindsey said. "He's a guy who wants to win, no matter what it takes. That showed when he was demoted and just went back to work as the offensive line coach. He could have looked for a job other places or he could have been bitter or complained, but all he cares about is doing whatever it takes to win."

No one appreciates that more than the boss who never wanted him to leave.

"We wouldn't have gone 13-0 without the way Hugh handled the situation—from the demotion to hiring a new coordinator and accepting the change in philosophy to the working relationship the coaches all had together," Tuberville said. "Al and Steve Ensminger also had to do their parts, but it took all three. The relationship couldn't have been better. All three of them are professionals."

CHAPTER 22

Georgia: Dawggone Good Time

When the third-ranked Tigers returned from their open date and reported for the team meeting on the Sunday before the Georgia game, the players and coaches came back physically and mentally rested, recharged and ready for the challenge that awaited them.

"We needed it bad," tailback Carnell Williams said. "We had such a long stretch from two-a-days right into the season and then nine games without a break. We had a lot of guys limping around playing with all sorts of bumps and bruises, and the open date really helped us get our legs back and come back stronger."

While the Tigers took a break from game action they didn't catch much of a break when they turned on their televisions to watch college football. By this point the national championship race was starting to dominate most college football conversations, and that conversation included Auburn.

Like the college football analysts who wondered whether or not Auburn could find a way to move past USC and Oklahoma, the Tigers found themselves asking the same question. When the team met on Sunday afternoon, head coach Tommy Tuberville didn't waste any time trying to move past the subject.

"If we drop one of these games coming up, it doesn't make a difference anyway," Tuberville said. "We're not going to talk about the BCS, because I can sense the guys were starting to put some pressure on themselves about it."

FIRST THINGS FIRST

If the Tigers needed any help focusing on the task at hand all they had to do was watch films of No. 8 Georgia, the defending SEC East champion led by the senior Davids—David Greene at quarterback and David Pollack at defensive end.

"To me Auburn's got a lot more riding on this game," Georgia coach Mark Richt said, playing coy. "They have a legitimate shot to play for the national championship if they win it. We're playing for possibilities and they're playing for real, tangible things."

The Tigers were also playing for intangibles, such as pride and bragging rights. For the Georgia natives on Auburn's roster, like cornerback Carlos Rogers of Augusta, playing Georgia "is like a championship game."

That's why the coaches weren't overly concerned about the Tigers losing any momentum during the open date. Offensive coordinator Al Borges addressed the realistic possibility of a flat start against Georgia by saying, "this team has done a really good job of coming out ready to play the game. This game and the rest of the season, I don't think that is going to be a problem."

If the first practice of the week provided any indication, the Tigers would be ready for the Bulldogs.

"They are relaxed, joking around, having fun," Tuberville said. "This group has had fun all year. They've been focused when they need to be and had fun when they needed to. I don't want them out there just grinding it out and taking all the fun out of it."

BIG BIG FUN

Of course there's nothing more fun than winning, and the Tigers came out loose and ready to win instead of playing not to lose. After Georgia drove 11 plays and 61 yards for a missed field goal, Auburn came right back with an eight-play, 80-yard drive that reached the end zone when quarterback Jason Campbell waited until the last second, took a hard hit and flipped a perfect option pitch to Carnell Williams for a one-yard touchdown.

Georgia's Pollack finally changed the momentum by blocking a punt in the second quarter, giving the Bulldogs the ball at the Auburn 29, but Rogers seemed to fly in out of nowhere to intercept Greene's pass to the end zone, turning the game back in Auburn's favor.

The Tigers responded by driving nine plays and 80 yards, finishing with a flurry on a trick play Borges had been hiding up his sleeve for weeks. It was a halfback pass, a play designed to let Carnell Williams fake the sweep, lure the pursuit in his direction and pass over their heads to receiver Anthony Mix.

"We practiced that *all year*," Williams said. "Me and Anthony Mix kept telling the coaches, 'We need to throw the halfback pass.' Finally in the Georgia game my number got called in the huddle and I told Mix, 'This is it, Mix, touchdown.'"

It wasn't a cocky thing. Instead, it was a Georgia thing.

"I knew it was a touchdown right when Coach Borges called it, because we kept running the sweep and their safeties and their linebackers kept crashing down," Williams said. "Coach Borges called it at just the right time."

Williams took the toss from Campbell and did his part, stretching the pursuit toward the sideline before raising his arm to pass. As he let go of the ball, the Georgia defenders swarmed him.

"I got flattened, but like all the great quarterbacks, I waited until the last minute to throw the ball and I saw him catch it," Williams said.

What he didn't see was the final result.

"Once I saw all the guys running up," Williams said, "I knew it was a touchdown."

Williams saved his celebration for the sideline.

"I was high-fivin' with Mix and saying, 'We've been telling y'all all year to run the halfback pass, it's going to work,'" Williams said. "Mix was excited, the coaches were excited, everyone was excited, but I was really excited. My first touchdown pass."

Williams isn't likely to spend much time passing the ball in the NFL, but just in case anyone wants to know, "I'm two for two in my

"Like all the great quarterbacks," Carnell Williams waited until the last second to throw his touchdown pass against Georgia.
Photo by Todd J. Van Emst

career. I'm perfect," Williams said. "My track record as a passer is pretty strong."

Just in case.

DOUBLE TROUBLE

Williams also hurt Georgia as a runner, receiver and punt returner, accumulating 227 all-purpose yards on 19 carries, four receptions and four returns. Ronnie Brown did his part with 12 carries for 52 yards and led the team with seven receptions, 88 receiving yards and a touchdown catch.

"When you've got two guys like that you're playing against a team as athletic as Georgia, you'd better make sure they touch it," Borges said. "There is no ingenious plan. This is not rocket science."

Whatever it was, it led to a 17-0 halftime lead and a 24-0 lead early in the fourth quarter. Campbell was cool, calm and efficient, completing 18 of 22 passes for 189 yards and a touchdown. The defense, led by a much-improved secondary, never let the Bulldogs near the end zone again until just 2:13 remained in the game and held Georgia to 85 rushing yards, 279 total yards and its fewest points in six years.

"It was one of those games where everything fell together," Tuberville said. "I thought this game would come down to four or five points. I haven't seen a complete game—offense, defense and kicking game—played that consistently in a long time."

FUN? ONLY ON FILM

Still, the question remained: would Auburn's 24-6 victory over Georgia be enough to convince the voters to move the Tigers past the No. 1 Trojans and the No. 2 Sooners?

"We're ready to jump someone," Williams said.

Maybe so, but the Tigers only had one vote in the coaches poll. They would have to depend on the coaches and the media, including the national reporters who attended the game from *Sports Illustrated*, *USA Today*, *The New York Times*, *The Boston Globe*, *Newsday* and the *Los Angeles Times*.

"I'd hate to play us," Tuberville said in an attempt to sell his team. "I know people will be fair when they vote. This is a special team. They lay it on the line every week. They are dang fun to watch."

Tuberville didn't get any argument from Richt.

"When you get beat like that, the only thing you can say is you got whupped," Richt said. "If a beating like that is going to happen, at least be glad it's against the No. 3 team in the country. We were out-executed and out-coached. I knew Auburn was good. They look exactly like they did on film."

CHAPTER 23

The Coaching Staff: Built to Win

Auburn's success in 2004 may have surprised outsiders, but it was no accident. For head coach Tommy Tuberville and his coaches, this was the result of a long-term construction plan that started when Tuberville and five of his current coaches arrived from Ole Miss in December, 1999, and found cracks in the program's foundation. Rebuilding the program and turning it into a championship program would require more than a quick fix.

"People have short strings now, and you see coaches fired after two, three, four years," Tuberville said. "It's taken us a while to get our program to where we wanted to, because we've done it the right way. We've built a base solid from the ground up, we haven't taken any shortcuts, we recruit good kids, make them go to class, and you would hope the people looking at those situations would factor that in."

None of those factors seemed to matter when former Auburn University president William Walker prepared to pull the plug on Tuberville and his staff in November 2003.

"We had a president who thought we should win the national championship and we didn't," Tuberville said. "So we were going to be replaced."

No one had to tell the coaches. They didn't have to listen to the radio, read the message boards or answer the phones. They knew they were gone in the days leading up to the 2003 Alabama game.

"Unless you went through it, you just can't imagine," defensive tackles coach Don Dunn said. "It's probably tougher on the families, the wives and children, because they spend a lot more time together than even we do during the season. It's just unfortunate that it happened, because Auburn is a lot better place than that, and that should never happen. If you want to get rid of me, be a man about it and come and say: 'Hey, Don Dunn, you're not doing the job.'"

It got so bad that running backs coach Eddie Gran was already looking to get out of coaching.

"In my mind, we did not have a job," Gran said. "I was out of the profession. I never thought I'd say that, but I was already talking to people. I love Auburn and wanted to stay in the area. I was a little bit bitter at that time. When you are like that, your mind isn't working right. I love coaching, but when all that came down, I was done."

While the coaches pondered their future at Auburn, their boss did his best to stand tall.

"He was kind of the rock we all looked up to as coaches. He never wavered. He never faltered," defensive ends coach Terry Price said. "He never showed any signs of the things that were getting to him, and that was great for us as assistant coaches to look up to a guy like that. He deserves this season, because he's worked hard to get this program where it is today."

BUILDING A STAFF

No head coach ever does it alone. A smart head coach surrounds himself with a mix of excellent on-field coaches, strategists and recruiters. If he's fortunate, some of those coaches can handle more than one of those tasks.

Ole Miss fans weren't quite sure what they were getting after Tuberville hired a mix of no-name coaches when he got the job in Oxford in 1995. Then again, with NCAA penalties and probation gutting the program, Rebel fans couldn't be too picky. What they didn't realize is that Tuberville came to his Ole Miss interview with a plan in place and a list of coaches ready to follow him. He still believes that helped him get the job.

One of Tuberville's first hires at both Ole Miss and Auburn was a strength coach. "That guy is around your players a lot more than your head coach and assistants. You're not going to have a strong program if you have a tough coach in your weight room, and you have to give that guy full leeway. You've got to tell him, 'When those guys are with you, you're responsible for them and they're responsible to you. If you run one of them off, they know there's no second chance with me.' I never get a call from our strength coach [Kevin Yoxall]. He takes care of his own problems and our players work hard for him."

Yoxall was one of only two coaches Tuberville hired when he came to Auburn. Tuberville brought eight assistants from Ole Miss, hired Yoxall away from UCLA and retained defensive assistant Joe Whitt from the previous staff. Whitt has been at Auburn since 1981 under former coaches Pat Dye and Terry Bowden, and in addition to his experience as a recruiter, he's a hard-nosed veteran ball coach who earns the respect of his players. In turn, they play hard for him.

"I hope [staying at Auburn] has something to do with me as a person and the job I've done and the commitment I've made to young people that I've been able to stay here for such a long time," Whitt says. "I've made a commitment to this community, to this university, the people of this university and the young men on our football team."

Staying anywhere for any length of time in the coaching business is difficult. Of Tuberville's original eight assistants, Joe Pannunzio left to become the head coach at Murray State in 2000, and coordinators Noel Mazzone and John Lovett were fired following a 7-5 finish in 2001. Gene Chizik replaced Lovett as defensive coordinator and stayed until January 2005, when he left for the University of Texas. Bobby Petrino replaced Mazzone as offensive coordinator and left after one year to become the head coach at Louisville. Veteran assistant Steve Ensminger replaced Petrino as quarterbacks coach and moved to tight ends when Tuberville hired Al Borges to run the offense in February 2004.

That leaves Gran, Dunn, Price, offensive line coach Hugh Nall and wide receivers coach Greg Knox as the only holdovers from the Ole Miss staff.

Over time, those coaches have formed a close bond that goes beyond the office and the field.

Eddie Gran, left, is one of the five remaining assistants who
followed Tommy Tuberville from Ole miss to Auburn.
Photo by Todd J. Van Emst

"When you get into this business, friendship means everything," Nall said. "We're in a situation where we all have to lean on each other so much that the guys become something a lot more important than the guy down the hall. They're brothers."

BUILDING BETTER CHEMISTRY

The chemistry on Auburn's coaching staff is no accident.

"The No. 1 criteria for a successful coaching staff in college football is that you have to be together," Tuberville said. "You all have to believe in the same things. You have to work and live together. You have to be able to put in 15-18 hours a day together. If you're not on the same page you're going to have problems. You can have disagreements and arguments, but in the final say so, everyone has to be on the same page. If you have a group that does that and believes in what you're doing together, then you've got a chance."

It helps that the coaches on the Auburn staff work and play together, doing everything from participating in interviews for new staff members and other important decisions to hanging out together socially with families.

"We treat this as a business where the head coach and the coaches all do things together," Tuberville said. "Obviously I have to have the final say, but there also has to be a tremendous amount of unity within your staff. There has to be a family atmosphere, and if you don't have that then you're going to have problems that are going to creep up during good times and bad times.

"Most of these guys have been with me for 10 years, and we've been through some tough situations. We started two programs from the bottom up and we've won, and won consistently, and a lot of it is because this staff works together and believes in each other.

"We try to create a family atmosphere. We do things away from the office as much as we do at the office, with our families and cookouts and other things. I believe in that. I believe the more you get together away from the office the more you understand about each other. You're always going to have problems, just like any family, but when there's a bond you can work things out a lot easier if everyone understands each other more."

That staff chemistry and cohesiveness was evident following the 2003 season when Tuberville replaced Nall as offensive coordinator and moved Ensminger to tight ends so Auburn could bring in Borges, another coach who has fit well into Auburn's staff.

When Borges interviewed for the job, he looked for a boss and co-workers he could respect, as well as a situation that would allow him to be more than a football coach.

"You've got to have respect for authority," Borges says. "It doesn't matter who the head coach is, if he says, 'This is what I want,' then you do it and you go about your business. If you don't have respect for that authority, you won't make it in this business.

"I'm also looking for a guy who isn't going to work you into the ground. The hours are long enough as it is, but I'm not into burning the midnight oil and sleeping in your office. I've got a life, too. I'm not leaving at seven during football season, but I'm not leaving at 1 a.m., either."

Instead of undermining Borges, Nall and Ensminger and the other offensive assistants made sure he felt welcome on the staff. Borges, in turn, made sure their ideas were heard and valued. He even adapted to Auburn's offensive terminology instead of forcing everything to adjust to him.

"Ego is one thing that can ruin a coaching staff," Tuberville says. "You're going to have egos. Everyone's got one, but you can't have selfish egos.

"It only takes one guy on your staff that has any kind of ego where he's all about himself instead of the team, that guy's going to run your staff. I don't have it. I'm not going to have it. If I ever get any kind of feeling toward that, that would be a big reason for a change.

"This year's success is all about being unselfish, with both the coaches and the players buying into that."

BUILDING A TEAM

Auburn's exemplary team unity in 2004 is another result of construction over coincidence.

"It's a conscious effort, a conscious plan," said Price, a graduate assistant under Tuberville at Texas A&M in 1994. "We inherited a few players in 1999 who were nowhere close to being the kind of kids we recruited and coached in the past. Some of them were very talented athletes, but they weren't what we were used to dealing with.

"When we recruit kids, we tell them we're going to bring them into an environment where they're going to have a chance to win football games and succeed academically, but they're also going to be around a bunch of guys they're going to enjoy being around. If you bring a bunch of thugs and kids who aren't good kids into your program, you can't go into people's homes and recruit kids and make that promise.

"So we made a conscious effort, from top to bottom, every single coach, to recruit kids with character, not just kids with talent. That starts with the head man. Coach Tuberville insists on that and we all believe in that. When you've got nine guys on the same page recruiting the same kind of players, you are where we are now six years down the line—a team full of good players.

"That doesn't mean they can't be tough kids, too. There's no lack of toughness. These are tough kids who come from good families and have good character and understand what it takes to succeed."

With increasing limits on how much time a coach can spend with a recruit at his school or his home, most successful college football staffs have been forced to become better detectives when it comes to investigating every potential signee. It's a matter of talking to high school coaches, assistant coaches, counselors, principals, assistant principals, even high school opponents to get a better understanding.

When that happens the coaches don't feel so bad about taking a chance on a player, such as former standout linebacker Dontarrious Thomas, a relatively anonymous high school recruit who spent his summer at math camps and played at a small Georgia high school, or defensive end Bret Eddins, the son of a former Auburn player.

"Brett Eddins is a good example," Price said. "Brett wasn't ever going to be a guy who could run a 4.5 or vertical jump 40 inches, but he was tall, had a big frame and had a lot of potential, but he had played middle linebacker in high school and never played defensive end in his life. But he came from a great family of Auburn graduates, a great character kid who works his butt off. We never had a problem from him, and he's been a three-year starter and a leader for us."

RESPONSES AND REWARDS

The unity and the shared sense of purpose paid off when it appeared the Auburn coaches were on the way out at the end of the 2003 regular season. When the news broke about the infamous "Jetgate" incident in Louisville, the players were quick to rally around the coaching staff.

The response of the coaches in the face of adversity set the tone for the 2004 season.

"I thought the best thing that we did last year after all this stuff had happened was we sat down as a staff and made a decision between all of us that we were not going to look back," Tuberville said. "If these players were going to learn anything from this coaching staff about this, it is that they put it behind them and they didn't look back. And I told the coaches we were going to do that, we weren't going to have any hard feelings towards anybody because this is a business, we have a job to do, we can't worry about the past, we have to worry about the future. Our coaches have done a good job with that, and we've handled it exactly that way.

"And hopefully if our players learned anything from that it's, hey, these guys handled adversity and they never let it bother our plans for what we were going to do in the future. Because again, this is a business, and I understand sometimes you might have to go through some things like that, maybe not to that degree, but I learned from it myself personally. Did I want to go through that? No. But after it was over with, it was probably the best thing for this program, this university and everybody involved. I've talked to everybody involved in the situation, and we all agree that what's best for Auburn is to look forward."

For all the players learned from the coaches, the players may never fully understand the way their reaction inspired the coaches.

"Coach Tub didn't let us deal with that," nose guard Tommy Jackson said. "The whole coaching staff told us we didn't need to worry about them, we needed to go out and beat Alabama. How can you not love and admire that? We rallied behind Coach Tub and all the coaches because of the way they handled that."

Give the players the credit for carrying that attitude over to the season.

"The way the kids responded says more than anything we could say," Whitt said. "I remember a newspaper story early on, before we'd even played a game, with Carnell Williams and Ronnie Brown saying, 'Lean on me. Here we go. We'll make it right for you.' This team sort of epitomized that attitude. The kids did that."

When the season finally came to an end, only to be replaced by award season, Tuberville won several national coaching awards from *American Football Monthly*, Walter Camp, the Associated Press, the Fellowship of Christian Athletes and the Paul "Bear" Bryant award from the National Sportscasters and Sportswriters Association.

The best award came from his peers in the American Football Coaches Association. Speaking to thousands of coaches in Louisville at the AFCA convention, just nine miles from the airport where "Jetgate" took place, Tuberville put the awards, and the season in perspective.

"This has been a team effort all year long, and this is a team award," Tuberville said. "It recognizes the job done by all our coaches and 123 great people on our football team who did everything we asked them to do."

CHAPTER 24

Alabama: Turning the Tide

As if playing archrival Alabama in Tuscaloosa wasn't motivation enough for Auburn, the frustrating stalemate in the polls and the Bowl Championship series standings gave the Tigers ample reason to circle the wagons and take on the world.

"We went into the Georgia week with everyone saying, 'If Auburn can beat Georgia convincingly they're going to jump Oklahoma,'" defensive end Bret Eddins said. "Then we did beat Georgia convincingly and everybody said, 'OK, let's see what happens against Alabama.'

"At that point we sort of figured nobody was going to vote us in. They just didn't want us in. Nobody really cared, either. We just decided to use it."

The Tigers did manage to climb into a tie with Oklahoma for No. 2 in the AP poll after the Georgia game, but they remained third in the coaches poll and third in the most important rankings, the BCS.

If the Tigers were feeling any additional pressure about their trip to Tuscaloosa, it certainly didn't show in practice that week.

"The one thing about this team is that they have fun," Tuberville said early in the week. "This team looks forward to going on the road. They'll enjoy going to Tuscaloosa."

Just the very idea of playing on Alabama's home field was enough to keep Auburn's attention focused on the task at hand. There are plenty of intense rivalries around college football, longstanding traditions such as Oklahoma-Texas, Michigan-Ohio State, Florida-Georgia, but people who know college football understand nothing compares to the relentless intensity of Auburn-Alabama, regardless of the circumstances surrounding the game.

"With it being Alabama and knowing how hard they're going to play and what kind of team they've got, you can't worry about the next game or think about different kinds of polls," tailback Carnell Williams said. "I'm just looking forward to the atmosphere. I know it's going to be crazy."

ABOUT HALF CRAZY

It actually got a little more crazy than most Auburn fans expect-ed—or wanted. While the Auburn offense produced minus-four yards on its first three possessions and wasted timeouts on successive plays on the second series, Alabama drove for a field goal on its first possession.

The situation could have been worse for Auburn if the defense had not come through on two Alabama possessions inside the six-yard line. First linebacker Kevin Sears intercepted a pass at the one-yard line to end a Crimson Tide drive. Four plays later Anthony Madison intercept-ed Jason Campbell, but the defense held the Tide to a field goal and a 6-0 halftime lead.

"In a potentially disastrous half we went into the locker room six points down, which was very favorable to us," defensive coordinator Gene Chizik said.

"The defense kept us in the game so we could win the game," offensive coordinator Al Borges said. "We put them in a hole a couple of times. The score could have been 21-0 at halftime. They kept turn-ing them back and giving us a chance to get on track."

HOW THE OTHER HALF LIVES

If the Tigers ever had an opportunity or a reason to panic, halftime at Alabama seemed to be a good time for it. Instead, the Tigers behaved as if they had been there before and knew just what to do.

"It was the first time we had been down at halftime all season but you couldn't tell in the locker room," strength coach Kevin Yoxall said.

Courtney Taylor's touchdown reception helped Auburn overcome a stubborn Alabama defense.
Photo by Todd J. Van Emst

"The kids were relatively calm and the coaches came out of their meetings calm and both coordinators talked to the kids about how they were going to fix it. There never was a sense of people ranting and raving and, 'What are we going to do?'"

Instead there was a plan to get the offense moving, and the Tigers did just that with the first drive of the second half. After an 11-yard completion to Courtney Taylor and two runs for 13 yards by Williams, Campbell finally broke Alabama's defense by connecting with Devin Aromashodu for a 51-yard completion to the Tide's five-yard line. One play later, Williams ran for a touchdown, and despite being outplayed for most of the first half, the Tigers led 7-6.

Auburn went on to take a 21-6 lead with 11:31 left in the game before Alabama answered with another score late in the game, but it was too late to prevent a 21-13 Auburn victory, an 11-0 regular season and the Tigers' 13th consecutive win.

"If I make it to heaven, I know this is what it's going to feel like," center Jeremy Ingle said. "We're the best team in America, and I'm not afraid to say it."

Go Get 'Em

That was an easy statement for Ingle to make, but not so easy for Tuberville to defend in his postgame press conference. Beating Auburn's archrival apparently wasn't enough. Winning by eight wasn't enough, either. Between the 6-0 halftime deficit and Alabama's late score, the Tigers found themselves trying to explain themselves to the media.

"This is the Iron Bowl and that's what it should be like," Tuberville said of the close game. "People will say, 'They struggled,' but most people who vote haven't been at this game before.

"Today, we didn't play perfect, but we found a way to win. This is one of those games where you'd rather people not watch it for style points. This is the Iron Bowl. This is not any other rivalry."

Even the Alabama players and coaches understood his point.

"As bad as this hurts me to say, I hope they win the national championship now," Crimson Tide quarterback Spencer Pennington said. "That's hard for me to say being an Alabama guy, that I want them to win, but they've got a great team.

"We realize that. They're going to do exceptionally well in the next two games they have. Go get 'em."

CHAPTER 25

Keeping the Faith: Brother to Brother

Spend 10 minutes with Tommy Jackson and it's not likely you'll see or hear a hint of the pain he carries in his heart. At first meeting he is a bubbly teddy bear of a young man with an inviting personality more prone to skipping this business of handshaking in favor of wrapping his six-foot-one, 300-plus-pound frame around you like a long, lost new friend.

Dig a little deeper and there's a pain that lingers from a lifetime without his father, a man who regrettably spent too much of his time imprisoned by jail and addiction.

It would have been easy for Jackson to let his father go, put up a permanent wall and move on, but Chette Williams wouldn't let Jackson off that easily. Williams, Auburn's team chaplain, pushed Jackson to let go of his bitterness and resentment and reconnect with his father.

"My dad and I have never really had the greatest relationship," Jackson said. "We weren't really that close when I was younger. He abused alcohol and drugs and he kind of abused my mom, so I had really bad feelings about my dad.

"If I go into the whole story it gets really long and hard to tell, but what I can say is that Brother Chette told me I had to give him a chance, and my dad and I were trying to work on our relationship.

"I can see that it was God really working in me now, because God was really putting it on my heart to get in contact with him, get closer to him, try to work these things out, be a Christian and forgive him like I should do.

"When my dad and I finally got together in the summer, we spent some time talking and trying to work things out, and we were talking outside my grandma's house when somebody shot a gun."

Jackson is not the kind of guy who goes looking for trouble, but trouble found him by accident that day. A heated dispute at the end of the street didn't even involve Jackson, his father or his young nephews and cousins, but a stray bullet from the confrontation soon became a personal problem for Jackson and his dad. Tommy Jackson Sr. was sitting in a chair when he heard the shot, stood up, moved instantly in front of his son and took a bullet through his stomach and liver.

Jackson's father managed to survive the shooting, but not without making an impact on his forgiving son.

"It's amazing how God works and moves," Jackson said. "My dad jumped in front of that bullet. If he hadn't been there, I might not be here. I could have been killed by random gunfire, but my dad jumped in front of me and took a bullet for me."

In November 2004, Jackson also lost his closest father figure when his uncle Fred Jackson died. Yet Jackson continues to exude a bountiful joy with his words and actions.

"Everything I've been through, if it hadn't been for Brother Chette, I wouldn't have survived," Jackson said. "Brother Chette helped me by helping me find God in every situation. There are times when you're sad and in pain and you don't realize that God is there, but He is, and everything happens for a reason. Brother Chette always helps me see that. If it weren't for Brother Chette, I don't know where I'm at."

THE RIGHT MAN FOR THE JOB

There are a significant number of people within the Auburn program who insist the Tigers would never have finished 13-0 and won the SEC without Chette Williams. The list starts with head coach Tommy Tuberville, who made hiring a team chaplain a high priority when he came to Auburn.

"This is a tough generation that we're coaching, these young men coming up now, because close to two-thirds of these young men don't have fathers," Tuberville said. "Every player needs a dad. They need someone to talk to, someone to relate to. Sometimes it's hard for them to do that with their position coaches. Sometimes they won't talk to a coach about their problems. Chette does that for them. He's made the biggest difference in our players' lives, my life, our coaches' lives, their families' lives than anything I've ever seen.

"We had a team of players who loved each other, believed in each other, and Chette had a lot to do with that."

Tuberville's decision to hire a team chaplain actually goes back to his first head coaching job at Ole Miss when he worked with the Fellowship of Christians Athletes to hire Wes Yeary as the team chaplain. According to Tuberville, "Wes became the most important person in our football program."

When Tuberville came to Auburn and Yeary stayed behind, Tuberville called Williams, who lettered as an Auburn linebacker in 1983-84. Williams was deeply involved in family ministry in Spartanburg, South Carolina, at the time and wasn't looking to move, but something clicked during his phone conversation with Tuberville.

"I really believed him, really trusted him right off the bat," Williams said. "I had no fear about it. I had such a peace about it, and I knew it was the right deal for me. I didn't know how it was going to work, because there wasn't a book on it, there was no blueprint.

"When I got off the phone with Coach Tuberville I told him I'd have to go home and talk with my wife and we'd have to spend a lot of time praying about this, so I went home to talk with my wife about the offer from Coach Tuberville. We had just started Impact Ministries in Spartansburg and it was going great and we had 200 volunteers, a staff of eight, a base of support, a bunch of kids we were involved with in the housing projects.

"When I got home I told my wife Lakeba about the job and said, 'I'll be a full-time spiritual coordinator. There's only one other job like this. I'll be one of the firsts. Plus, it's Auburn.' I told her, 'We're going to have to spend a lot of time praying about this, so I'm going to go into the bathroom and start praying and you go into the bedroom and start packing.'"

The baptism of Carnell Williams was one of many signs of
Chette Williams's impact on the Auburn football team
Photo by Todd J. Van Emst

Williams laughed as he delivered the punch line, but his message was clear.

"I was ready," he said. "Sometimes when God speaks, you just know it's right. I've never regretted it a single day."

A TIGER'S TRANSFORMATION

Williams wasn't always ready. In fact, after he walked on at Auburn in 1981, he barely survived his first two years because of his anger and destructive habits.

"I had a lot of anger and a lot of frustration coming from my home life," Williams said. "I left home with a bad attitude toward my father and the world."

Eventually, Williams found himself using a locker next to Kyle Collins, a white halfback from Gadsden. "He didn't really like black people, grew up in a racist environment," Williams said. "I didn't like him much, either."

Despite their differences, Collins still asked teammates in a Bible study to pray for Williams. Their response, Collins told the *Huntsville Times*, was, "'Hey, pray for somebody that has a chance.'"

Collins actually tried to break down their barriers by befriending Williams and trying to tell him about his faith, but Williams ignored him until the night assistant coach James Daniel came to Williams's dorm room and told him the coaches had decided they no longer wanted Williams and his bad attitude around the football program.

In his desperation, Williams went to see Collins and started asking questions.

"He started telling me about the love of Jesus Christ, how much Jesus loved me, how much God loved me, how God had a plan for my life and how that plan would work in my life, if I would just commit my life to God," Williams said. "That night we got down on our knees and prayed together, and my life changed forever."

Williams went to see Dye the next day and told him what happened. Instead of sending him home, Dye told him to stay and take it one day at a time.

"I'm still taking it one day at a time," said Williams, who graduated from Auburn and went to seminary in New Orleans so he could prepare himself to help other young men learn some of the same lessons he learned at Auburn.

"I've had kids come in here and had to personally tell them their parents were dead or had been killed," Williams said. "I've had kids come in struggling with all kinds of problems and addictions. I've had coaches come in struggling with separation and divorce. I've had kids come in here struggling with hate and other emotions. I've seen it from A to Z.

"At the same time, I've seen some of the best things happen, too. I've married players, baptized players, helped some of them come to know Jesus as their Lord and savior. I've seen players graduate. I've seen players go to the NFL. I've seen a lot of them leave here strong in their walk. I've seen some of them become good husbands and fathers, still strong in their faith."

At the same time, Williams knows he must be careful not to push his religion on every student-athlete who walks in his office. Williams takes a broad approach to his job, emphasizing his role as a counselor and mentor to anyone in need.

"I'm just trying to be available," Williams said. "I don't want to force Jesus on everybody. Jesus didn't force himself on me. He says, 'I'll stand at the door and knock, and if you answer, I'll come in.' I'm not going to do that to these guys. The only I'd accomplish is running these kids away."

BUILDING A FOUNDATION

Young men have enough problems these days without someone running them away. As an Auburn assistant since 1981, linebacker coach Joe Whitt has witnessed a tremendous shift in the culture young people grow up in.

"The more I look at it, it's not the kids who changed, it's us," Whitt said. "Society accepts things it didn't use to accept. We've become tolerant of certain things we didn't use to tolerate—the way we dress, the way we speak, the way we treat other, the way we work. When you accept a lower standard, it gets easier to accept a little more, then a little more, then a little more, and it just becomes the way things are done.

"So then we say we can't handle these kids because things aren't like they used to be. But what's changed? The kids? Discipline is still discipline. Yes still means yes. No still means no. So what's changed? It's all in what you'll accept and not accept. That's not the kids' fault. It's the fault of the adults making the decisions."

Part of Williams's job is to help players build a foundation in that shifting culture.

"Kids are different today in terms of how they were raised," Williams said. "A lot more Division I-A football players, especially in the SEC, were raised in single-parent homes, usually by single-parent moms, and sometimes by single-parent grandmothers. A lot of these kids are expected to be providers, and they become 'men' before they're ready.

"A lot of them were raised without a strong male figure and never learned to respect a male authority figure, except maybe their high school coaches. In a lot of cases they have a negative vision of male authority figures because their fathers left their moms and have never been there for them.

"That may seem far-fetched for a lot of people, but there are a lot of football players in the SEC who don't even know their dads. Then you bring them here to college where most of their authority figures are men, and you're going to have some conflict there. To get them to respect those male authority figures, to get them to trust and believe in those people, to convince them that what that coach is saying or doing will make them better on and off the field, that's a big key for these young men.

"That's why it's so important for us to deal with those issues. We have to deal with the character issues, the mental issues, the spiritual issues. The athletic ability is there. Most of them are ready physically to play Division I-A football when they come here, but they aren't mature enough. They aren't ready mentally and spiritually, and it's our role to help put all those pieces in place."

Williams has been at Auburn since 1999 and the Tigers have offered some kind of team devotional or FCA program for years, but Whitt has never seen those pieces come into place like they did in 2004.

"This group is different from any group I've ever been around," Whitt said. "You ask why and I'd say one reason is Chette Williams. I mean that with all sincerity. I've watched guys go through changes that are just unreal, guys you'd never thought would become real witnesses, and they witness with conviction. He's done a great job."

CROSSING LINES

Something must be working, because the players are devoted to Williams and each other. How else you do explain 60-70 players at a time gathering for Bible study and prayer on a Tuesday night during the summer?

During a time when the players are attending summer school, working summer jobs and pushing themselves through demanding workouts in the Alabama heat and humidity, "We had Brother Chette pulling us closer and closer together," cornerback Carlos Rogers said. "Once that bond formed we never broke it.

"He's not just a guy who's going to be a chaplain and give us the word on things and just be religious. He's the kind of guy where you can go into his office and he really helps you put things in the right perspective. He helps you know where to go. He's been a big help to so many people on this team—not just the guys he preaches to or the guys he's baptized—but guys who just needed someone to talk to and someone to guide them down the right path."

Those Bible studies also helped the players break down racial, economic and geographic walls. That unity was best exemplified when several greenhorn hunters, both white and black, urban and rural, accompanied experienced outdoorsmen Rhett Autrey and Tim Duckworth on a December hunting trip.

"Tim and Rhett knew what they were doing," Jackson said, "but the rest of us, we're all just out there farting around. I'm just thinking, 'If I see anything, I'm gonna shoot.'"

The rookies behaved like typical novices, making noise, laughing, telling jokes and falling asleep when they should have been moving through the woods in cautious silence.

"We didn't know any difference," Jackson said. "Marcus McNeill was out there snoring real loud, and Timmy was getting all mad at us, giving us dirty looks."

Despite the total lack of woodsmanship displayed by his teammates, Duckworth finally saw a deer, only to have his teammates all jump up and start shouting and getting ready to shoot. Duckworth and Autrey, of course, left the woods empty-handed that day, but it hardly seemed to matter.

"Timmy's black and Rhett is white, but they're like best friends ,because they're both country boys and they have something in common, while the rest of us were more city guys. Marcus is from Atlanta. He's never been in the woods," Jackson said. "But we were all out there finding something in common about each other, trying to learn more about each other. We were all able to go out there and enjoy each other's company.

"With this many guys, we're bound to have a lot of different opinions and things like that. We have guys from all walks of life, but this team is not about color or where you're from. Everybody tries to love each other and respect each other and be teammates. It's like a family."

SINGING SOLDIERS

Auburn's growing team chemistry carried over to the season and found a defining moment the night before game at Tennessee when tight end Kyle Derozan first sang "Hard Fighting Soldiers" for his teammates at a team devotional. The song repeats the line "I am a hard fighting soldier on the battlefield" and makes references to Ephesians 6:11 in which the Apostle Paul writes, "Put on the full armor of God." The song also refers to Psalm 60:12, which reads, "With God we all gain the victory."

"That song has always stood out to me, and every week we're in a battle with opposing teams," Derozan said. "At that meeting Brother Chette asked me to sing that song with the team and we could use it as a motto."

That night the Tigers started hooking arms in prayer like Roman soldiers walking into battle. By the Ole Miss game, they were singing "Hard Fighting Soldiers" in the postgame locker room. By the Sugar Bowl, they were walking onto the field, locked arm in arm in a show of unity.

"One thing about this team is that we felt like God had His hand on everything we did," Jackson said. "By that being said, I mean working hard and believing everything you do will pay off and work out the way God wants it to."

Some religious people believe in a deity that directs every event and every moment, even the results of a football game. Some believe in a creator that allows free will and human strengths and weaknesses to control the outcome of a sports contest. It's easy to debate the relative merits of the various theologies and philosophies of Auburn's chaplain, coaches and players, but it would be missing the point.

The Tigers never said God loved them more than their opponents and controlled the outcome of every play and every game. To put it simply, the players spoke of a two-way relationship involving faith and trust that became more real to them through time and experience.

"Brother Chette let us know that God was always there, and He would never leave us, even during tough times," Jackson said. "Sometimes life isn't easy, even for believers, but God is still there. We learned to understand and accept that because of Brother Chette. I guarantee you we wouldn't be the same team if it weren't for him."

CHAPTER 26

The SEC Championship Game: The Dandy Dozen

Despite a 21-13 road victory over archrival Alabama on the previous Saturday, Auburn still slipped to third in the AP poll and remained third in the coaches poll, although they picked up more first-place votes in both polls. The Tigers received eight first-place votes in the AP poll, two more than the previous week, and received four first-place votes from the coaches, two more than the previous week.

It was during that period, in the two weeks between the Alabama game and the SEC championship game against Tennessee, that the unforgiving reality of Auburn's realization hit home: unless Notre Dame could beat No. 1 USC or Iowa State could beat No. 2 Oklahoma in the Big 12 championship game, the Tigers would most likely be left out of the national championship picture, even if they defeated Tennessee.

Still the Tigers refused to back down or give up. They had a chance. That would have to be enough as they prepared to play Tennessee.

"We should be the top one," head coach Tommy Tuberville said, "but I'll take two."

WHO'S NO. 2?

As if the Tigers needed any extra motivation to win the SEC championship, they found it in Knoxville. In the two weeks between games, they were reminded time and time again about the comments of Tennessee linebacker Kevin Burnett after Auburn's 34-10 victory over the Vols on October 2.

It was Burnett who sat straight faced after that one-sided game and insisted, "The best team out there today was Tennessee."

Perhaps Burnett saw something everyone else missed, including Tuberville.

"You've got to go by what the score is," Tuberville said with a laugh. "I don't know how other teams play. We normally go by who has more points at the end of the game."

Then to add a little salt to the wound, Tuberville added: "I don't know what number Kevin Burnett is, but I'm sure he made some plays."

When Tennessee players such as Burnett and free safety Jason Allen refused to back off their comments before the SEC championship, it added a little extra fuel to the game.

"We see in the papers posted on our board that they're still not giving us any respect," tailback Ronnie Brown said. "I'm excited about playing them again and giving them an opportunity to come out and prove themselves."

As for the Tigers, they had their own point to prove to the 15th-ranked Vols, as well as a national television audience.

"People, for some reason, don't expect Auburn to be at the top," quarterback Jason Campbell said. "A lot of [people] are just waiting for us to fail. A lot of people still don't give us credit for the season we've had."

Including, it seemed, Burnett.

"[Burnett's] had a big mouth all year," Auburn center Jeremy Ingle said. "That's the way he is. There's certain people like that who can't cope with the fact that they got beat on a certain day. That's fine. He'll have his shot again."

The Tigers took their SEC championship celebration
to the stands at the Georgia Dome.
Greg McWilliams/Icon SMI

TIME WELL SPENT

While the Vols struggled to get past Kentucky and Vanderbilt in their final games of the season, the Tigers went home for four days and enjoyed Thanksgiving dinner with their families. It was a gamble by the coaches to let the players spend so much time away, but the team's maturity and work habits made it a gamble worth taking.

The move paid off when the Tigers returned on Friday and went right back to work. "It was good," Brown said. "It gave everybody a chance to go home and relax and chill with their families and get their minds away from football for a week."

The Friday return, however, did give the Tigers some extra time to prepare for the Vols.

"They've seen some of the things we've done, so we'll probably have to mix it up a little bit," Brown said. "We may have to spread them out a little more and get some down-the-field plays to the receivers to get them softened up on the defensive side of the ball."

A LASTING LEGACY

Brown proved to be all too right. Campbell had not thrown more than 27 passes in a game all season, but when the Vols insisted on committing their defensive plan to stop the run, Campbell responded by throwing 35 passes and hurting Tennessee with an impressive 27 completions, 374 yards and three touchdowns.

Even when the Vols bounced back from a 21-7 halftime deficit with two quick touchdowns for a 21-21 tie, it was Campbell who put the Tigers back on track with a stunning strike.

With the Tigers desperately in need of a big play, Devin Aromashodu didn't waste any time or moves on Tennessee's secondary. He blew right past cornerback Roshaun Fellows and Allen on a deep route, and Campbell did his part for a 53-yard touchdown pass.

"It felt like the play was in slow motion, because I knew I was open and I had to wait on the ball a little bit," Aromashodu said. "I thought the ball would never get there. I just wanted to make sure I caught it, because I knew we needed a big play."

Campbell followed with an eight-yard run for a first down on a drive that produced a field goal and a 43-yard touchdown pass to Ben Obomanu for a 38-28 victory.

"He showed his character," offensive coordinator Al Borges said. "He could have gone in the tank and lost it. Our kids didn't lose it. They don't do that."

With Campbell winning the game MVP honors, the Tigers also moved to 12-0 for the first time in school history and won the program's first SEC title since 1989. For the seniors, many of who were redshirts when Auburn played in the SEC championship game in 2000, winning the SEC would leave a lasting legacy.

"I hope this becomes a regular thing for this program, like Tennessee, Florida and Georgia," defensive end Bret Eddins said. "A lot of teams expect it. We've kind of been like the bridesmaids in the West being co-champs a couple of years and only going one time.

"We've been close, just haven't been able to take that next step, so hopefully things will work out for us. A lot of seniors have SEC co-champ West rings. A lot of guys have worked through stuff. It will mean a lot for the whole team, coaches, fans, everyone—not just me and these seniors."

'WE'RE THE BEST'

Only one accomplishment could mean more than an SEC championship.

"We definitely deserve a chance to play for the national championship," Campbell said. "We've done all we can do. We've done what people asked."

In the giddy, emotional moments following the game, the Tigers quickly turned their thoughts to the final BCS standings to be announced the next day. USC and Oklahoma had taken care of their own business, so all the Tigers could do was plead their case to the media and hope for the best.

"It's hard to go 9-0 in the SEC and 12-0 undefeated," Campbell said. "To play a team like Tennessee twice, to beat them twice, it's hard to do. You think when you do that you'll have a chance to play for the national championship."

Tight end Cooper Wallace said, "My belief is the SEC is the hardest conference out here. The others are good, but people have to look at what we've done in this conference—going undefeated and winning the championship. I think we deserve it."

Tuberville added, "All you have to do is look at our record. Some people say we didn't play as tough a schedule, but we played four teams that won nine games. We're the only one that did that out of the top three teams. I just hope they look at it fairly."

Despite their pleas for a fair shot, the Tigers knew it was a long shot.

"It's going to be very difficult," defensive end Stanley McClover said. "I hope the voters do right and put us in the Orange Bowl."

And if they didn't?

"We're the best team in the nation, we think," cornerback Carlos Rogers said. "If they don't vote us in, we'll be ready to play whoever comes our way."

CHAPTER 27

The Seniors: Leading the Way

As 18 seniors neared the end of their time at Auburn, head coach Tommy Tuberville couldn't help reflecting back on the fifth-year seniors who joined the program in February 2000.

"We were selling a dream," Tuberville said. "Things weren't real great around here at the time. That's what you have when you're building a program back."

Tailback Ronnie Brown believed, switching his commitment from Tennessee to Auburn. Quarterback Jason Campbell believed, choosing Auburn over Georgia. Defensive end Bret Eddins always believed, but he grew up in an Auburn family, the son of a former Auburn player. Strong safeties Junior Rosegreen and Donnay Young and linebacker Mayo Sowell had other options and chose Auburn. Kicker Phillip Yost grew up in Auburn, but he was a *USA Today* All-American with other choices.

"Coach Tuberville is a very charismatic guy," Eddins said. "We believed in him and we believed in ourselves."

The other fifth-year seniors—center Jeremy Ingle, holder Sam Rives, offensive tackle Rich Trucks and safety Bret Holliman—walked on at Auburn, just looking for a chance.

They were joined a year later by a recruiting class that included tail-back Carnell Williams, cornerback Carlos Rogers, guard Danny

Lindsey, defensive tackle Jay Ratliff, linebacker Derrick Graves and receiver Silas Daniels, six players who never redshirted. Two years later they were joined by a junior college transfer, defensive end Doug Langenfeld.

Together, those 18 comprised a senior class that left an indelible mark on the Auburn football program, not just as players but as people.

OUT OF THE FIRE

When the Tigers emerged from the ashes of a turbulent 2003 season, it was the seniors who followed Tuberville's lead, bought in with a purpose and paved the way for their younger teammates. The first big step came when Williams, Brown and Rogers all decided to pass up the NFL Draft and return for their senior seasons.

"Those guys not going pro and coming back and being as unselfish as they were throughout the whole situation," Eddins said, "... It's just hard to imagine where we'd have been without them."

By the time August came around and two-a-days began, the seniors knew something was different about this team.

"I could tell during the summer workouts," Campbell said. "The coaches aren't here, and it's up to us to go out there on our own and we're out there doing seven-on-seven drills. This year's seven-on-seven was a lot different than any other seven-on-sevens I've ever been a part of. Guys were really serious about it.

"I think a lot of it had to do with what happened last year and all the seniors we had coming back. We had a lot of seniors stepping up and leading and a lot of young guys willing to follow.

"It started in the summer and then carried over into two-a-days. We had great two-a-days. Guys were going at it. It was more competitive than it's ever been."

It took a special level of commitment to make the summer a turning point for the team.

"We had player meetings all summer where the older guys got together with the younger guys and just worked on the little things so we'd be that much further ahead when we started practice," Eddins said. "It's kind of tough in the summer to leave an afternoon pool party and come up here and go through a bunch of drills and work with the younger guys.

"It's not like you didn't want to do it, but it's summer time and you're just hanging out, being lazy, and one guy would say to another, 'OK, it's time to go,' and everyone would climb into their cars and come to work. It's one of those deals you just have to do if you want to be great, so it all paid off. It was all worth it."

The coaches have heard it all and seen it all before, so they waited for the actions to speak louder than the words they were hearing, but they soon came to see something special emerging as the season opened.

"This group was unique, because as a coach, no matter what level you're on or how much you coach, you always preach team," defensive end coach Terry Price said. "This is the first team I've ever seen truly become *a team*.

"I'm talking about guys sharing responsibilities, working together, not caring who gets the credit or who gets the most reps. Everyone's just been happy to be part of a winning team.

"There's an old coaches saying, 'It's amazing what happens when nobody worries about who gets the credit.' That's been true for this team."

The coaches didn't have to look very far to find the primary reason.

"I think the biggest reason has been the senior leadership after last year," Price said. "The seniors took charge of this football team and made sure the younger guys understood after those tough times we experienced last year that a team has to be stick together, in good times and bad times. They took charge of things, so I give all the credit to our seniors."

MAMAS, DADDIES AND YOUNGINS

While we're at it, how about a little credit for the people who raised those seniors?

"So many of our families know each other," Eddins said. "A lot of parents come to all the games, and my mom would hug and kiss all the players as they came out after the locker room after every game."

Auburn's seniors and their head coach came
together through struggle and success.
Photo by Todd J. Van Emst

Carnell Williams's mom took her team-first devotion to another level. Sherry Williams paid a visit to a sporting good store in Gadsdan in September, before the LSU game, and had the store make her a special Auburn jersey. She wanted Ronnie Brown's No. 23 on the front of the jersey, because, as she told the *Huntsville Times,* "Ronnie was at Auburn before Carnell. When Carnell got to Auburn, Ronnie showed him everything."

She had Carlos Rogers's No. 14 put on one shoulder and backup running back Tre Smith's No. 22 on another shoulder. She followed with Jason Campbell's No. 17 on the sleeves. The back was reserved for her son's No. 24.

"If I had room," she told the *Times,* "I'd put all their numbers on there."

Her son couldn't have been more proud of her—or the other parents who supported their sons.

"It goes to show you what kind of players and parents we have here," Williams said. "Most of the time you take your lead from your parents, and my mom did her part to help show what kind of team we are with her jersey—Ronnie's number on the front, my number on the back, Jason's number on the side. She's not just supportive of me, she's supportive of the whole team. She wants to see everyone do well.

"That's the kind of attitude we had on this team. We didn't want one or two guys to get all the glory. We wanted the collective group to get the glory from winning."

IT'S LAUGH OR CRY

Anybody who's ever been around a team knows you have to have a thick skin to survive, because the humor and pranks can seem cruel to outsiders. Yet they're really just part of the give and take of being part of a family.

"The camaraderie and the sense of humor were amazing, the way the guys could joke about stuff," Eddins said. "Things other people might get offended about, you'd have guys just laughing and shaking it off like it's no big deal.

"A lot of that comes from last season, because we took so much abuse. You couldn't go anywhere without being told you suck and people getting mad and asking, 'What's wrong with y'all?' We had to learn to take it for what it's worth. Really it brought us closer together and made us more of a family."

This was definitely a group that knew how to have fun, even if it came in the heat of battle. The seniors often instigated it, but even when the underclassmen started it, the seniors went along.

"People talk about the receivers and the DBs getting on each other, but with us, the offensive and defensive linemen were the most vocal about getting on each other," Eddins said. "We're just joking around but I've had friends come out to practice and say, 'I thought y'all were about to fight.' I'd just laugh. If you fight with someone on our team, you're going to have to fight with everyone."

That feisty sense of humor at practice never kept the Tigers from getting their work done, but it sure made practice more enjoyable.

"It was a lot more relaxed this season," Eddins said. "We were serious when we needed to be, but it's really a lighthearted group that knows how to have fun.

"Guys would wear the wrong number to practice every other day just to make a joke out of it. Some guys would dress like each other and imitate each other at practice. Will Herring and Andrew Letts switched uniforms at practice one day and they were running like each other and doing impressions of each other. It was scary how well they could imitate each other.

"We had guys out there imitating coaches. Everybody imitates Coach Price because his voice gets really high when he gets excited. Junior does a good imitation of Coach Price when he calls people 'big fella.'

"Kevin Sears does a dead-on imitation of Coach Whitt, but he won't do it in front of Coach Whitt. He won't do it much around anyone. He's too scared of Coach Whitt. Jake Slaughter does a pretty good imitation of Coach Gran. Most everybody can do their coach because they're around them so much, you sort of pick up on their little mannerisms."

LEON COMES TO AUBURN

Have you seen the Budweiser commercials featuring Leon, the fictional star football athlete? In the baseball commercial, Leon's on his cell phone in the on-deck circle, referring to himself in the third person and talking about getting paid for his public appearances instead of getting ready to bat. In the football commercial, he's in the locker room after a loss, refusing to take any blame for his part. A reporter asks, "You don't think your four fumbles played a part in the loss?" Leon responds, "Not if those guys fell on the ball. Once again, Leon can't do everything!" When the reporter says, "There's no 'I' in team," Leon answers, "There ain't no 'we' either."

Of all people, Brown became "Leon" on and off the practice field, even taping the name "Leon" on the back of his jersey and pretending to emulate Leon's conceited persona.

"Ronnie's as far away from Leon as you can get, so that's what made it even funnier," Eddins said. "One time I was sitting across the room during interviews when a reporter asked him about the Tennessee game, 'How did it feel when you fumbled in the Tennessee game and they got the ball?'

"Ronnie just looked at him real serious and said, 'Man, Leon can't do everything, somebody else could have jumped on that ball,' and just got up and started walking away. The reporter was just sitting there wondering, 'What the heck?'

"After about five or six seconds Ronnie came back in and just starting laughing. Then he sat down and gave a serious answer about how you don't want to hurt your team by fumbling, but for a few seconds he really had that guy."

THE ODD COUPLE

What happens in Vegas stays in Vegas, but that's not always the case in the apartment Carlos Rogers and Carnell Williams shared. They became roommates in 2001, despite co-existing more like Oscar and Felix from "The Odd Couple" than two future NFL stars.

According to Williams, Rogers is "more of a pretty boy that watches TV and loves to shop. He's kind of like a woman. He's so clean and things like that, and he loves to shop. I've never met another man that loves to shop, but he'd rather shop than do just about anything."

Rogers got his turn to respond in public at the annual Senior Watch Banquet in Birmingham.

"He was talking about rooming with Carnell and having to tell Carnell to pick up his underwear and socks off the floor and having to take Carnell to Wal-Mart to get his Noxema and all his skin-care products," Eddins said. "He took some shots at Carnell, and the guys were just rolling."

Rogers has often taken credit for getting Williams to dress better, but Williams denied it.

"Nah, I'm not a big dresser. I haven't picked up any habits from Carlos," Williams said. "When I want to dress nice, I can. But he dresses every single day. That's just not me. I just don't have the type of money he's got to buy clothes."

RAISING 'EM UP THE RIGHT WAY

The seniors did more than just lead by example and voice. They also became mentors to the younger players.

"I see freshmen coming in here and they are all excited," Rogers said. "They come in and the first thing they see is Coach Yox [strength coach Kevin Yoxall]. They want to leave. They want to ask why he is so hard. I tell them he has a lot to do with what you are going to do in the future, that he will help you train your body for what you are going to do on the field. It's hard for them to understand. It was hard for all of us."

One of the best examples of mentoring came from the defensive line when redshirt freshman Quentin Groves needed help surviving the summer of 2004.

"There was a time in the summer when Q was struggling real bad and wanted to quit," Langenfeld says. "He was struggling with the defense, the concepts, the move from defensive end to linebacker to defensive end.

"I told him if he quit and took the easy way out he'd be a coward and he'd always quit. I told him he had to stick it out because he had so much ability and so much talent, if he just kept plugging and learned how to use it. I told him it would pay off in the end and it did."

Groves responded by becoming a key player in 2004, finishing tied for the team lead in sacks and tackles for losses.

"During the summer, the seniors wouldn't let us take the easy way out," Groves said. "They'd always push us the extra mile, whether it'd be in minicamps or during workouts or running. They'd always tell you, 'You can't give up now. In a game, you can't lay down. On third-and-long, when you want to get after the passer, you can't get a break. They ain't going to call timeout because you're tired.'"

Groves obviously got the message. Near the end of the season, Langenfeld left Groves with a new message.

"It's like I told Q: 'Hey, this is your team now. I'm just on this team for a few more games and after that my career is over. We just laid the foundation, but for the next three or four years, it's y'all's team and you've got to carry on,'" Langenfeld said.

A FINAL TRIBUTE

It's become an Auburn tradition to carry the seniors off the field after their final on-campus practice before the team leaves for a bowl. On that day in December 2004 the Tigers found themselves in a reflective mood.

"It really hasn't crossed my mind that I'm not going to be working out with Yox," Campbell said. "I remember the sled, the hill and the 5:30s. Those are the things that you remember the most, the hard work together as a team and pushing each other with icicles on the ground. Being out here at 5:30 in February flipping and rolling together. Those are the things you remember the most."

The underclassmen did more than carry their leaders off the field that day. They also left fitting tributes with their praise.

"It seems like they've been seniors ever since we've been here," junior wide receiver Ben Obomanu said. "Ronnie, Jason, Carnell and Junior have kind of been the vocal leaders for the young guys since I've been here. It's going to be kind of sad to see them leave."

The seniors left to follow new paths, but not without leaving a map for their teammates to follow.

"We've been through so much, but they're the ones who helped us move to the next level," sophomore noseguard Tommy Jackson said. "They used their experiences to show us that we can overcome adversity and still be OK and walk tall and keep our heads high no matter what happens. They've been an inspiration to so many of us and taught us how to be leaders and how to love each other.

"We really tried to build a family and that's what we've done. We're not going to lose that just because a bunch of guys are leaving. They don't want us to lose that. They did all they did for a reason. They want us to keep building a dynasty in football but they also want us to keep building a family here, guys who love and care for each other, and that's what we're trying to do."

Junior receiver Courtney Taylor added, "They taught us how to deal with adversity and come out on top. With all they've been through, to come back out and have this type of year and keep their heads high and keep everybody positive says a lot about them. You got guys like Carnell and Ronnie—two guys who could have won the Heisman this year if they hadn't shared the position, but they were so unselfish about helping this team win.

"That really carried over to a lot of guys on this team. You can see that kind unselfishness all around the table on this team. They transferred all that to us so now we need to teach the younger guys the way they taught us. We understand this is the key to winning, the key to success. If you love winning, you'll do the things they taught us and pass it on to other guys."

The seniors soaked it all in, but like the players and people they had become, they weren't about to let it deter them from their final goal of winning the Sugar Bowl and finishing 13-0.

"I know we will be missed," Rosegreen said. "It's our time to pass the torch to the upcoming seniors. We want to end on a good note."

CHAPTER 28

The Sugar Bowl: Bittersweet Perfection

Auburn's concerns over its place in the national championship race proved to be well founded. The day after the Tigers beat Tennessee in the SEC championship game they came up short for the first time all season, with the BCS sending USC and Oklahoma to the Orange Bowl for the national championship.

Auburn, on the outside looking in, would play Virginia Tech in the Sugar Bowl for a chance to finish 13-0 and a slim chance to crash the national championship picture. In any other year, playing in the Sugar Bowl would be a sweet experience for the Tigers. This time, it tasted a little sour.

"We're honored to be in the Sugar Bowl," quarterback Jason Campbell said, "but in our hearts we still feel like we should be playing for the championship."

While head coach Tommy Tuberville was quick to insist the BCS "needs a little bit of work," he was just as quick to move his team forward instead of dwelling in disappointment.

"There are a lot of people that have national polls . . . *Golf Digest* has one . . . *Outdoor Life*," Tuberville joked. "We can't do anything more than what we've done. We're going to keep doing what we've been doing and enjoy what we've accomplished and go down and enjoy the reward these guys have earned.

The BCS couldn't stop Jason Campbell and the
Tigers from celebrating their perfect season.
Chris Graythen/Getty Images

"We've been trying to convince the AP voters to look at us for several weeks, but we haven't done a very good job of it yet. But maybe everybody won't make up their minds until they see how the bowls go.

"We'll just go down to New Orleans, have a good time and see what happens."

LOOKING AHEAD

A good time? In New Orleans? Telling a bunch of college guys to have a good time in New Orleans is like playing with fire near a gas pump. Tuberville and his coaches quickly defined their version of a good time by telling the players to be careful about how much time they spent on Bourbon Street and other French Quarter night spots. Even walking the streets at night, they insisted, could hurt a team's legs in the days leading up to the game.

The seniors insisted they would keep the younger guys in check and make sure they stayed out of trouble and got to bed on time.

"New Orleans is one of the party capitals of the world," senior center Jeremy Ingle said. "I've already set limits on myself and what I'm going to be able to do. I don't think I'm going to be going out much after the 29th or 30th, because this is too big of a game. We can't lose this game. We've got too many seniors on this team and too much going for us to go out and blow it by going out and partying every night."

Bret Eddins learned about such things as a little boy, joining his family at the 1987 Sugar Bowl. Before his father, Liston Eddins, took his team out on the town he warned his sons Blake and Bret about the dangers of Bourbon Street.

"I told them, 'There are topless women down there, so I don't want you looking in those windows,'" Liston said. "One of them asked, 'You mean they don't have any heads?' I didn't miss a beat. 'No, they don't, and it's horrible.'"

BACK ON TRACK

Mid-December brought a number of individual awards, with Carlos Rogers winning the highest honor—the Thorpe Award as the nation's top defensive back. Numerous other players won a variety of awards, with running backs Carnell Williams and Ronnie Brown, quarterback Jason Campbell, offensive tackle Marcus McNeill, strong safety Junior Rosegreen, linebacker Travis Williams and nose guard Tommy Jackson all earning first-team all-SEC honors and Tuberville winning SEC Coach of the Year honors.

Those awards did nothing to satisfy the Tigers. If anything, the awards only made them more intent on proving themselves as a team. By the time they completed semester exams and returned to the practice field, their hard feelings had not softened.

"It takes something out of you when you have commentators talk about how Auburn should just accept it and just move on," Campbell said. "It's not something you just accept. You work hard to get to this point. You think about all of the hard work and everything we've done this year to get the opportunity to play in the Orange Bowl, and somebody just talks about 'just accept it.' That means they really don't respect you that much as a team.

"We just feel like we are at the point now where it doesn't matter what we say or do, because we won't be playing in the Orange Bowl for the national championship. That's just how it is. We also understand that people can't take away what we've done this year, and what we've accomplished. We also feel like we still have an opportunity to be the co-national champions."

With that in mind, the Tigers returned to work to prepare for Virginia Tech.

"You have a lot of players that are upset," safety Junior Rosegreen said. "When we come back to practice, it's up to us as seniors and upperclassmen to get their minds right for this Virginia Tech game."

Those seniors shouldering the responsibility of taking care of their younger teammates in New Orleans would have to set the tone throughout the month of December, especially in practices and meetings.

"We'll lean on our seniors to help get these guys ready like we have all year," Tuberville said. "They've been ready for every game, and they'll be ready for this one. They understand this will be one of the better teams they've played all year. Virginia Tech is going to be ready to go. We want to make sure we are prepared to play our best."

Virginia Tech also helped the Tigers get their heads on straight in mid-December. Watching the Hokies on film convinced the Tigers they were in for a fight with a tough 9-2 team that suffered two near-misses against No. 1 USC and North Carolina State.

"That's one reason why we're not talking a lot about the BCS—because we're playing a Virginia Tech team in my mind that should be undefeated," linebacker Travis Williams said. "They should have beat USC but they got a bad call. They got inside the 20 against North Carolina State and shanked a field goal. At the end of the season they have been playing the best football of any team in the nation."

THE FINAL CHAPTER

The Tigers found out just how good Virginia Tech could be, but not until the second half of their game in the Superdome.

Campbell once again led the way on offense, hitting tight end Cooper Wallace for a 35-yard reception on Auburn's first offensive play. On the next series he converted on third-and-16 by connecting with

Courtney Taylor for a 23-yard gain across the middle. Those big plays and three Jon Vaughn field goals gave the Tigers nine first-half points and the defense, due in large part to a dramatic stand that held the Hokies scoreless on four plays inside the Auburn two-yard line, held Tech scoreless in the first half.

When the Tigers improved their lead to 16-0 with 10:39 left in the third quarter on a five-yard touchdown pass from Campbell to Devin Aromashodu, the Tigers appeared to be making a strong case for their national championship argument.

However, two fourth-quarter Virginia Tech touchdowns cut into Auburn's one-sided dominance before the Tigers put the finishing touches on a 16-13 victory and a 13-0 record.

"We dominated the game for three and a half quarters," Campbell insisted. "You can't look at the final score and judge us by that, because if you were at the game and watched the game, you understood how we dominated the game."

"We didn't worry about beating people by 40 points," Tuberville said. "It's about winning by one point. We did get conservative. That was my call. It worked tonight. It worked all year long."

Maybe so, but would it be enough to convince voters the Tigers were better than either the Trojans or Sooners?

"Two teams play tomorrow night and it will probably be a good game," Tuberville said. "Neither one of those teams is better than we are. We'll play them anytime, anywhere. Somebody will make us national champions, and that's all we want."

UNFORGETTABLE

Instead of playing the Trojans or Sooners, all the Tigers could do was lobby for votes. They started by storming the ESPN Gameday stage after the Sugar Bowl, imploring voters to give them a chance and doing everything they could to justify their place in the national championship debate.

"We were trying to make our case," Campbell said. "I think, at Auburn, we have to be our own lawyers. People need to understand we played a heck of a schedule. I hope the AP voters understand we fought just as hard as anyone. It's not our fault we're not in the national championship game."

The next day, Campbell took his best shot in an attempt to sway any undecided voters.

"To go 13-0 for the first time in school history, to go undefeated in the SEC, to beat a team twice [Tennessee], this team more so than ever deserves a national championship," Campbell said. "Our defense did a great job. They haven't given up [more than] 20 points but one time all year long, and USC and Oklahoma have given up 20 or more points at least twice. Offensively, we've been consistent all year. We've done what we've had to do to win games all year, we've made plays, and just sitting back and looking at it, we were consistent as far as winning, and the closest games we had were [against Virginia Tech], probably the Tennessee game [in the SEC championship game], and the LSU game."

Later that day at the Orange Bowl, Tuberville said, "You shouldn't have to campaign. There's no doubt that we've done all you can expect someone to do: play good teams, beat the ACC conference champion who's in the same conference with Miami, Florida State, Virginia and Georgia Tech. We really don't have to campaign. Somebody's going to pick us, but for some reason, we don't get a lot of respect.

"You get overwhelmed sometimes when you're ranked high early, but high rankings early don't make a difference. It's how you play during the year and how you finish up. This is a strong team, a great team, doesn't get any better. I can remember in 1991 at Miami when we won the national championship and Washington also won somewhere else to split the national championship. It should be that way, because if you don't have a playoff, you should have an opportunity to have a share of it. Why not? They ought to give it to Utah and everyone who is undefeated."

It was all Campbell and Tuberville could do. They couldn't prevent Southern Cal from whipping Oklahoma 55-19 later that evening in the Orange Bowl. USC finished No. 1 in the polls. Auburn finished No. 2, moving ahead of Oklahoma. Later that week, the Tigers would receive national championship recognition from the *Eufaula* (Alabama) *Tribune* and the People's National Championship, an on-line fan poll based in Opelika, Alabama, and Tuberville promised his players would receive national championship rings.

Still, the taste of bittersweet perfection lingered.

"I don't think anybody can tell me to my face we're not national champions," Campbell said. "We deserve it. I'll show our ring. I'll show it to USC, Oklahoma. They can show me theirs and I'll show them ours. We may have to make our own trophy. That's OK."

Given a choice, the Tigers would have preferred one more game.

"Bring 'em on," Carnell Williams said, referring to USC. "The neighborhood park would be fine."

"No doubt," Rosegreen said. "We beat four of the top 10 teams in the country. We went undefeated in the SEC and then we won the SEC Championship. That should speak for itself. We'll play them anytime, anyplace, anywhere. If they really wanted to do it, after they played their game we could play them the following week. For the national championship, anybody would get ready if you're a football player and you have any pride in yourself. We would be ready to play them."

Who's to say they wouldn't have been ready? Who could say they wouldn't have won? The Tigers lined up 13 times in the 2004 season. The Tigers won all 13 games. They won with confidence, character, unity, unselfishness, hard work and all the things that make a team special. Not winning the national championship will always be something of an asterisk at the end of the season, but no one and nothing will ever change the fact that Auburn did everything it had to do to earn a perfect season.

"We've got a lot of heart. We've got a lot of want-to. We've got a lot of integrity," Rosegreen said. "I think we'll never, in this world, find another team better than us, because we do a lot of things together. We pray for other teams when a man gets hurt. We'll pray for him just because that's what kind of character we have. We just knew at the end of the tunnel it was going to be a good season for us. That's why we just kept going and were able to go 13-0.

"There's no doubt in my mind we left a legacy. They will never forget us. That's what it's all about."